FLORIDA'S FINEST INNS AND BED & BREAKFASTS

Text, photographs, and art by
Bruce Hunt

PINEAPPLE PRESS, INC.
SARASOTA, FLORIDA

DEDICATION

THIS ONE IS FOR RUDI AND COCOA (see back cover) and especially for my mom, Gerry Hunt—without all her help I never could have finished this book.

Pineapple Press, Inc.
P.O. Box 3899
Sarasota, Florida 34230

www.pineapplepress.com.

Library of Congress Cataloging in Publication Data

Bruce Hunt, 1957–
        Florida's finest inns and bed & breakfasts / Bruce Hunt.—1st ed.
                p.   cm.
        ISBN 1-56164-202-9 (alk. paper)
  1. Bed and breakfast accommodations—Florida—Guidebooks. 2. Hotels—Florida—Guidebooks. 3. Florida—Guidebooks. I. Title.

TX907.3.F6 H86 2001
647.94759'01—dc21

                                                        00-062344

First Edition
10 9 8 7 6 5 4 3 2 1

Design by Carol Tornatore Creative Design
Printed in the United States

ACKNOWLEDGMENTS

THANKS TO THE MANY owners and managers—too many to list—who sat on front porches, in parlors, and at kitchen tables to talk to me about the joys, the labors, and the rewards of owning, operating, restoring, and living in Florida's finest inns and bed & breakfasts.

Special thanks to my girlfriend, Loretta Jordan. The places in this book are meant to be shared with someone, and sharing them with her made them all the more special to me. Thanks to my aunt Bonnie Corral, who is such a terrific promoter of my books, and to the wonderful crew at Pineapple Press, particularly Kris Rowland for her thoughtful and thorough editing.

CONTENTS

Northeast Region

Central West Region

Central Region

Central East Region

Southwest Region

Southeast Region

INTRODUCTION

SEVERAL YEARS BEFORE MY wrting career began, I fell in love with Herb Hiller's *Guide to the Small and Historic Lodgings of Florida,* an award-winning Pineapple Press publication so popular that it was printed in three revised editions, the last one in 1993. I bought stacks of them and gave them away as Christmas and birthday presents. I have never met the man, but he inspired me to write this book.

Writing *Florida's Finest Inns and Bed & Breakfasts* seemed a natural extension of the work I had done writing and researching *Visiting Small-Town Florida* Volumes 1 and 2. While working on those two projects, I regularly came across historic inns and beautifully restored homes that had been converted into bed & breakfasts, and I always felt compelled to write about them. I did write about them but it was necessarily abbreviated coverage, since those two volumes were intended to be books about small towns, not about inns and bed & breakfasts. So I was delighted when Pineapple Press gave me the go-ahead to do this book. I already had a great list of places that I wanted to include, and I knew of plenty others that I was anxious to research.

Books evolve as they are being written. This one certainly did. You'll find *Florida's Finest Inns and Bed & Breakfasts* to be quite different, in many ways, from other lodging guidebooks. Oh, don't worry. The descriptions and all the pertinent information are here—rates, amenities, contact information—but for some of the places, I've chosen to dig a little deeper. In cases where I found a story or a place's history compelling, I have gone into some detail (and sometimes I throw in a good restaurant recommendation). For instance, in the section on Miami Beach, I have covered its early history, its recent restoration and the controversy that surrounded it, and Art Deco architecture in general. Because of my keen fascination with history and architecture, my descriptions and discussions lean in those directions. To paraphrase something that I pointed out in my last book, *Visiting Small-Town Florida,* Volume 2: knowing the history of a place makes it infinitely more interesting to visit.

This is not a collection of all of Florida's inns and bed & breakfasts. When I first began my research, I felt that the lodgings should meet some criteria: they should have a minimum of six rooms, have private baths, be non-smoking, have been in business for at least three years, and not be chain hotels. Most of the places listed in this book fit those criteria, but I kept coming across marvelous exceptions that I didn't want to exclude. Initially, I also wanted to cull out the very large hotels, but then I couldn't bring myself to leave out some of Florida's grandest and most historic inns, like the Belleview Biltmore, the Don Ce Sar, the Biltmore in Coral Gables, and the Breakers. In retrospect, I can see that it was impossible to choose the entries using such quantitative criteria. Eventually I decided to trust my instincts and choose them on their individual merits. The result is a collection of wonderful Florida accommodations, all 135 of them worthy not just as places to stay, but as interesting destinations as well. They are many things— quaint, historic, romantic, eclectic. Some are haunted, and all are certainly exceptional.

There's something else you will find here—stories about people who decided to change the course of their lives, about following a dream, about hope, about walking into an old, dilapidated house and seeing the beauty that used to be there and having the passion to be willing to spend many times more than its appraised value to restore it.

I hope you enjoy this book. And I hope you use it to occasionally get away from it all—something that I feel is as necessary as sleeping, eating, and working.

A TALE OF TWO HENRYS: FLORIDA'S GRAND HOTELIERS

IT'S IMPOSSIBLE TO DISCUSS historic Florida inns without talking about the two Henrys, Florida's grand hoteliers and railroad magnates, Henry M. Flagler and Henry B. Plant. At the turn of the twentieth century, these two men separately but simultaneously turned Florida's east coast and west coast, respectively, from virtual wilderness into civilization.

I have mixed feelings about Henry Flagler. Every time I drive down I-95 through south Florida, I curse him. He's the one who opened the floodgates for all this mayhem—this frantic mass of humanity and all the tackiness, traffic, crime, and aggravation that goes with it. It's insane! Sometimes I think south Florida is just one giant nine-thousand-lane-wide boulevard wedged between the Atlantic Ocean and what's left of the Everglades. Thanks a lot, Henry!

But the more I read about the man, the more he fascinates me. His accomplishments in Florida would be astounding if performed today, but eighty, ninety, a hundred years ago, they were positively superhuman. And Flagler did nearly all of this at an age when most people are rocking on the front porch at the Shady Rest Home! He was a genius, he was a visionary, and he was the consummate philanthropist. Although for much of his life he was driven by an insatiable thirst for prosperity, none of what he accomplished in Florida was motivated by profit. It couldn't have been—he lost a fortune! Flagler was a brilliant businessman, but Florida was not about business to him. It was about creativity. The east coast of Florida was Flagler's blank canvas, and his railroad tracks, through and over impossible terrain, and his castlelike hotels were his art.

Henry Morrison Flagler, a preacher-farmer's son, left the family's farm in Hopewell, New York, when he was only fourteen years old. Even at that age, he understood that he could not be satisfied with the meager life that awaited him if he stayed. He made his way to Republic, Ohio, to work for his older half brother, Dan Harkness, at L. G. Harkness and Company, a general store founded by Dan's uncle. Henry was a determined worker, and although his formal education had ended after the eighth grade, he quickly developed sharp business instincts and showed a natural talent for salesmanship. At thirty-two, he invested his life's savings, with a partner, in a new salt mining venture. Initially they made money, but at the end of the Civil War the salt market collapsed, and so did their business. Henry went to work for a grain merchant company, Clark and Sanford, in Cleveland. It was in Cleveland where he and John D. Rockefeller became close friends. At thirty-seven, Henry joined Rockefeller's fledgling firm, Rockefeller and Andrews, which three years later would become the Standard Oil Company.

Flagler had married Mary Harkness, one of L. G. Harkness's daughters. The Flaglers lived on the same street as the Rockefellers and Samuel Andrews, the third partner in their firm. The three worked closely together, but Rockefeller and Flagler were particularly tight.

Petroleum was an emerging product and new uses were being found for it all the time. In their first two years, the company tripled production. Flagler quickly evolved into the contract and negotiations man, negotiating very favorable railroad rates by guaranteeing minimum volumes per day. This gave Rockefeller, Andrews, and Flagler a distinct advantage early on in this new industry. Soon the smaller competing refineries around Cleveland weren't able to make any money, so Flagler, representing the firm, began buying them out. Naturally he acquired them at discounted prices.

In January 1870, in order to be able to sell stock and generate more capital, the three partners incorporated under a new name, Standard Oil Company. In later years, someone asked John D. Rockefeller if that was his idea, and he responded, "I wish I'd had the brains to think of it. It was Henry M. Flagler." Standard Oil continued to gobble up the little guys, even the tiny ones that were producing only a barrel a day. Within months following its incorporation, the company owned eighty percent of the refining volume in and around Cleveland, and its owners were gaining a reputation for ruthlessness. Many of the complainers, who had had little choice but to sell their refineries to Standard Oil, had done so for combinations of cash and stock in the company. The sellers may have been unhappy at the time, but those who hung on to their Standard Oil stock ultimately became quite wealthy.

The growth of the Standard Oil Company was phenomenal. It spread to the Northeast, acquiring more refineries and forming alliances with others. Flagler used Standard Oil's might to negotiate more special rates with railroad and pipeline companies. In 1879, the Standard Oil conglomerate and its associates—known as the Standard Alliance—controlled ninety-five percent of the U. S. petroleum industry. Flagler's official title was secretary. His real job was dealmaker.

The Standard Alliance had caught the attention of Congress. In 1882, the

Alliance became the Standard Oil Trust, the largest business concern in the United States. The public wanted it broken up; it was too big and exercised far too much control over oil, rail, and other related industries. Federal investigations and hearings took place continuously over the following decade.

Henry Flagler took the stand and was grilled many times, saying as little as he could but always contending that the company's success was simply the result of hard work and smart business decisions. He and his partners fought as long as they could. Finally, by direction of the United States Supreme Court, the Standard Oil Trust was dissolved in 1892. However, as liquidating trustees, the Standard Oil group still maintained what amounted to monopolistic power. Not until 1911 was Standard Oil truly dissolved— into thirty-five different companies.

The Flaglers had moved to New York City in 1877. Mary Flagler's health had been declining for many years. In the winter of 1878, they took a trip to Jacksonville, Florida. Mary's health improved marginally, but sadly, in May 1881, she died. This staggered Henry. He had been a very devoted husband and father to their two children, Harry and Jennie Louise, but he had also spent a great deal of his time consumed with the business. Now he took a different look at his life. That summer he moved the family to Satansoe, an estate at Mamaroneck on Long Island Sound. From then on, he steadily tapered back his involvement with Standard Oil and spent more time with his children. Flagler was still secretary and still owned stock, but he gradually had less to do with the company's day-to-day operation. Of course, he didn't need to work. By now he was infinitely wealthy.

In June 1883, Henry Flagler remarried. His new wife, Ida Shrouds, had been Mary Flagler's nurse in her last, declining years. Not everyone was as excited about the marriage as Henry. Ida was eighteen years younger than he, reportedly short-tempered, and a compulsive shopper. Perhaps she was after Henry's money? They delayed their honeymoon until December, when they traveled to Florida, eventually making their way to St. Augustine. Henry was enthralled with the town but was surprised at the lack of development. They stayed for two months, which was plenty of time for the wheels to start turning in Flagler's head.

Two years later, Henry and Ida returned to St. Augustine. A new hotel, the San Marco, had opened, and there were some other new developments as well. St. Augustine was just starting to wake up. Boston architect Franklin Smith had built his Spanish Alhambra-style residence out of a new building material that combined cement and shells. Smith mentioned to Flagler his interest in building a hotel. Flagler, too, was beginning to like the idea of building a hotel. In March 1885, the city held a celebration honoring Juan Ponce de León's landing on Florida's east coast. Perhaps it was the romantic sound of that name, but Henry Flagler's first decision regarding his hotel was that it would be named the Ponce de Leon.

Flagler had just become acquainted with Dr. Andrew Anderson, well known in St. Augustine. Anderson owned quite a bit of property in the middle of town, and Flagler bought some of it before heading back to New York. When he returned in May, he convinced Dr. Anderson to act as his local representative in the building of the Ponce de Leon Hotel. By December, workmen were breaking ground. Flagler liked Franklin Smith's new cement-and-shell building material (a forerunner to concrete) and chose it for the Ponce de Leon. It took over a thousand workers at a time to mix in the coquina shells, pour the cement, and pack it into the forms. The walls were solid-cast and four feet thick.

The 450-room Spanish Renaissance Ponce de Leon Hotel spread across five acres. More than an architectural marvel, it was (and still is) an enormous and magnificent piece of sculpture. It was designed with fountains, statues, towers, domes, balconies, stained glass, a seven-hundred-person oval-shaped dining hall, and the detailed craft work of artisans that no one would even consider taking on in a hotel project today.

From the start, the process took longer than anticipated. Part of the problem was transporting materials to the site. The narrow-gauge Jacksonville, St. Augustine, and Halifax River Railroad (which ran from Jacksonville to St. Augustine) was woefully inadequate, so Flagler simply bought it and immediately instituted improvements. The fifty-five-year-old, recently retired Standard Oil tycoon had begun the second half of his life with two new avocations: hotelier and railroad baron.

Some of Henry's old Standard Oil pals thought perhaps he had spent too much time in the Florida sun. These were incredibly expensive and very risky projects. Flagler was undeterred. He bought the Casa Monica Hotel in 1888 (a year after Franklin Smith completed it) and renamed it the Cordova. In 1887, he began construction on the Alcazar Hotel—across from the Ponce de Leon and next to the Casa Monica/Cordova Hotel. The Alcazar was to be an intimate and less-pricey alternative to the Ponce, which finally opened in January 1888.

Today the Ponce de Leon Hotel is the main structure on the campus of Flagler College, and the Alcazar contains the Lightner Museum. The Casa Monica/Cordova Hotel had been an office building for years. In 1999, it was remodeled—one of the most elegant hotel restorations I've seen—and resurrected once again as the Casa Monica Hotel (see St. Augustine chapter, Casa Monica Hotel).

In March 1889, Flagler's daughter, Jennie Louise, died following complications from childbirth, during which her child also died. As a monument to her, Flagler built the Venetian Renaissance Memorial Presbyterian Church one block from the Ponce de Leon Hotel. Both she and Henry are buried in the mausoleum there. His philanthropic pursuits in St. Augustine were many and included rebuilding the Catholic Church after an 1890 fire and building a hospital in 1889. He was also the major contributor responsible for building City Hall and an African-American school.

Flagler continued to acquire railroads. By the end of 1889, he had purchased an assortment of small rail lines, connected them, and improved them—in many instances adding bridges where ferries had done the job before. His railroad now extended as far south as Daytona. Along the way, he bought a small hotel in Ormond Beach. For a while he thought that this was as far as he would go. South of Daytona the coast was mostly wild swampland with just a few small settlements. Plus, there were no existing rail lines to buy up. He did, however, own some steamers that ran up and down the Indian River, and they were doing fairly well transporting citrus.

Flagler was not one to remain idle for long, and soon he got the itch to expand south. In 1892, he got his state charter to build railroads down as far south as Miami (although he claimed he had no intention of going that far). This was going to be a more formidable undertaking. Until now he had acquired and improved on existing rails. Now he would be building a railroad from scratch, much of it through uncharted wilderness.

Construction started in June 1892. By November, workers had reached New Smyrna. The next leg, to Lake Worth (and what would later become West Palm Beach), was more difficult. Swampland had to be filled in before the tracks could be laid. It took a year and a half to get there. A month before the railroad arrived, Flagler had already completed, in record time, his largest hotel yet. This one had 540 rooms and was constructed of wood. He called it the Royal Poinciana, and it sat on the east bank of Lake Worth. At the time it was completed in February 1892, it was the largest wooden hotel in the world. Two years later, he opened a second hotel on the beach a half mile east. This one, the Palm Beach Inn, was smaller and simpler. Patrons began referring to it as The Breakers since it was down on the beach where the waves were breaking. (See Palm Beach chapter, The Breakers, for more information on this hotel.)

Palm Beach turned into precisely the kind of resort-for-the-wealthy that Henry had envisioned. It was a crowning achievement. Once again, he did not anticipate going any further south, but a lady with an orange grove on the Miami River changed all that.

In 1893, widow Julia Tuttle, who owned considerable acreage in what is now downtown Miami, offered to split her property with Flagler if he would bring his railroad all the way down to Miami. Flagler passed on the offer. Two years later, a devastating February freeze wiped out nearly all of central and north Florida's citrus. Julia Tuttle seized the moment and sent Flagler a cutting of fresh, healthy orange blossoms from her groves, along with a reminder that her offer still stood. Oranges were probably the biggest commodity being shipped north on Flagler's rail cars and Mrs. Tuttle's message hit home this time.

Flagler's railroad arrived in Miami in 1896, and he wasted no time in constructing the palatial Royal Palm Hotel, a smaller version of his Royal Poinciana Hotel. In the summer of 1899, Miami suffered a deadly outbreak of yellow fever. The city went under quarantine in October, which added economic disaster to a town already devastated by the epidemic. During the five-month quarantine, Henry Flagler hired those who were healthy but confined and out of work. They built sidewalks, roads, and whatever needed improving. As long as they could find something to work on, Flagler sent them money. No one went hungry, and the town of Miami benefited.

Henry Flagler was a much-loved man, not only because of the boom that he almost single-handedly created, but also because it was apparent that he genuinely cared about and took care of the people in the communities that he developed. But public opinion was about to turn on him.

Two years before Henry began developing Miami, he started noticing some odd behavior in his wife, Ida. At first he didn't discuss it with anyone. Then their New York family physician, Dr. George Shelton, told him about a bizarre and delusional conversation Ida had had with him. Not long after she learned that she was not able to bear children, Ida told Dr. Shelton, among other things, that she had in her possession magic stones, one of which could cure a barren woman. Her mental state continued to deteriorate after that. Henry was distraught and felt powerless to help her. Her delusions became more pronounced and more frequent. She became convinced that she was in love with the Czar of Russia and that he was in love with her, even though they had never met or communicated. She proclaimed she was destined to marry the Czar as soon as Henry died, which she predicted would be soon. This news came to her via her Ouija board. She also experienced sudden fits of rage without warning. At one point she locked herself in her room, claiming that spies had infiltrated the house and were after her. Ida had been under her doctor's close observation for nearly a year when it was suggested that it would be best for her to be committed to Choate's Sanitarium in Pleasantville, New York.

After eight months, the doctors at Choate's thought Ida had improved enough to go home. Having her back thrilled Henry, and he went to great lengths to entertain her at their Mamaroneck home. She seemed fine for about a month, then relapsed into her previous state of insanity, once again obsessed with the Ouija board and convinced of her impending union with the Czar of Russia. Her doctors became concerned that she might actually try to kill Henry in an attempt to fulfill her delusion. Henry hired many specialists to help Ida. They recommended that she return to the sanitarium, but Henry didn't want to send her back there. When she became dramatically worse, he hired Dr. Du Jardins and four nurses to care for her full-time at home. At the doctor's recommendation, Flagler moved into a Manhattan hotel and was advised not to see her. Ida's condition worsened. Her violent tantrums grew more frequent. She now lived in a fantasy world in which her husband was dead and the Czar of Russia was going to take her away. In March 1897, she was re-committed at the Pleasantville Sanitarium. Although for years he sent Ida flowers every week, Henry never saw her again.

Two years later, in 1899, Flagler moved his residency from New York to Palm Beach, Florida. Some speculated that it was because a divorce was easier to obtain in Florida. At that time, even in Florida, insanity was not a valid reason for divorce. However, in April 1901, a bill went before the Florida State Senate and then the House that would change that, making "incurable insanity a ground for divorce." It passed easily and Governor Jennings signed it. Immediately, newspapers labeled the bill the "Flagler Divorce Law." Few doubted that Henry Flagler had wielded his influence to have the law changed. He didn't do much to hide the fact, either. Two months later, he filed for a divorce from Ida; in two more months, the state granted it. One week after that, Flagler announced his engagement to North Carolinian Mary Lily Kenan. Even more sensational was the fact that Mary Kenan was less than half Flagler's age. Most people were highly critical of Flagler, but his close friends stuck by him.

In Flagler's defense, he had set up a trust made up of cash, Standard Oil stock, and property for Ida. Overseen by a trustee, it was worth well over two million dollars. Her annual income, beyond the expenses of keeping her at the sanitarium, was roughly $100,000 per year. Ida, who had by now completely disconnected from reality, knew none of this. Her trustee eventually moved her to a private cottage on the grounds of another sanitarium, where she lived the remainder of her life.

Another tumultuous chapter in his life had passed, and an aging Henry and his young bride were living full time in Palm Beach. Aging or not, Henry Flagler had one more monumental task to perform, and this one would be his most audacious.

Even before Flagler's railroad had reached Miami, there was speculation that he might attempt to build an extension all the way down to Key West. The idea captivated him, but he was not going to rush into it. Building a 150-mile-long railroad that would skip across tiny coral islands but would mostly be elevated over water was something that had never been done. It was something that many claimed couldn't be done. When the green light was given to dig the Panama Canal, Flagler knew the time was right to build his overseas railroad. Key West would be the nearest rail terminal to the canal by three hundred miles.

In 1904, Flagler extended his rail line from Miami down to what is now Homestead. Flagler and his engineers discussed at length where to go from there. One option was to jump from Cape Sable in the lower Everglades straight down to Key West, but the final choice was to follow the Keys. Construction began on Flagler's "impossible folly" in the summer of 1905. His engineers predicted it would take three years to reach Key West. It took seven. A work force of three thousand men labored almost non-stop. It was a logistical nightmare. Rail cars brought huge tanks of fresh drinking water in daily. Much of the equipment to drive pilings and pour concrete at sea had to be fabricated just for this job.

In October 1906, the concrete bridge trestles were put to the test during a violent hurricane with winds that topped 120 miles per hour. The trestles survived, but seventy men in camps built on barges died. In 1909, another huge hurricane struck. With the men now housed in sturdier lodgings, all survived. The engineers were convinced that the bridge trestles were hurricane proof, but not the train sitting on top of them. So they devised an electric switch that automatically stopped the train before it crossed a bridge if wind sensors detected a velocity of fifty miles per hour or greater.

Finally, on January 22, 1912, the first official train arrived in Key West with eighty-two-year-old Henry M. Flagler aboard. The arrival was a grand affair, attended by U. S. politicians and representatives from many Central and South American countries and from Cuba, as well as the entire population of Key West. More trains followed throughout the day. One had come straight through all the way from New York. Florida Governor Gilchrist arrived on the last train. Key West celebrated for days. Henry Flagler had accomplished what nearly everyone had declared impossible.

Fifteen months later, on May 20, 1913, Henry Morrison Flagler died quietly at his home in Palm Beach. No specific cause of death was listed. Newspapers reported simply that he had died of sheer exhaustion.

While Henry Flagler was taming Florida's east coast, Henry Plant was doing the same on the west coast.

Henry Bradley Plant learned about overcoming adversity at a very young age. He was six when his father, sister, and aunt all died of typhus. Henry also contracted the disease but managed to survive. When he was eighteen, Henry went to work for the New Haven (Connecticut) Steamboat Company as a deckhand on steamers that made the run from New Haven to New York City and back. In 1842, he married Ellen Blackstone and, in 1852, they had a son, Morton Freeman Plant. Henry changed jobs so he would not be away from his family. He went to work for the Adams Express Company, an express delivery business. It was here that he developed his business acumen. Hard work and natural talent landed Henry numerous promotions. In 1854, when Adams bought out a delivery company in Georgia in order to expand, Henry was put in charge and the Plant family moved to Augusta.

The Southern division of Adams Express did well under Plant's direction. Delivering everything from currency for the United States Mint to newspapers, this division had established connections with every steamship port and railway terminal in the South.

In April 1861, just four days before the first shots of the Civil War were fired at Fort Sumter, Plant met with executives from Adams and offered to buy out the Southern division. War was imminent. The executives weren't going to be able to keep the division anyway (because they were headquartered in the North), so they accepted his offer of $500,000 in notes. Henry named his new company Southern Express. Because of Henry's relationship with the Adams people, Southern Express was the only major delivery company in the South that was able to transport packages to the North. Sometimes they even handled North-South prisoner exchanges.

Adversity was preparing to test Henry again. As Union troops moved down into the Southern states, they took away Southern Express's connections one by one. Then, Ellen Plant died of tuberculosis. Doubly devastated, Henry took a sabbatical. When the war finally ended, he began to put the pieces of his company back together. Adams Express had picked up most of his connections taken over during the war, and they returned them to Southern Express—after all, Adams executives were still holding Henry Plant's note.

Southern Express had always made its deliveries to railroad terminals. From those points, the railroad companies carried the packages to their destinations. One of Plant's competitors thought he would try some vertical integration and buy a railroad, the Mobile and Ohio. When he failed to make a go of it, Plant stepped in and bought the railroad from his competitor for a bargain basement price.

Henry Plant was now in the railroad business—and he was good at it. Southern Express prospered and did particularly well transporting produce, citrus, fish, meat, and other perishables from the South up to the North.

Before long he paid off his Adams note, and his focus shifted to railroads.

Plant's genius was in acquisitions—recognizing potential in an existing operation (that was usually in poor financial shape), purchasing it for a considerable discount, and then building it into a profitable venture. He did it again when he bought the bankrupt Charleston and Savannah Railroad, the Florida Southern Railroad, and the Atlantic and Gulf Railway, which he bought at public auction. Next, he diversified into steamships and connected them with his rail terminals. Plant's interconnected transportation system was opening up Florida's citrus, vegetable, and lumber markets to the rest of the country.

Henry Plant had long dreamed of providing a regular transport link between Florida and the West Indies (the Caribbean)—especially Cuba. He had been to Cuba and saw great promise there in transporting goods and people. Tampa Bay and Charlotte Harbor were his two favorite choices for ports. He went to Tampa first.

In 1883, Plant purchased the land grants and rights-of-way granted by the State of Florida to the Jacksonville, Tampa, and Key West Railroad (which was running out of money before track could be laid) for running tracks between Kissimmee and Tampa. The only problem was that the charter ran out in seven months. Plant got the seventy-five miles of track down in just over six months.

At first, because Tampa Bay was so shallow, steamers had to anchor out in the bay, and smaller launches would unload freight and passengers. So construction began on Port Tampa in 1888. Docks were built. Rails were run to the docks. Channels and basins were dredged. Plant spent more than three million dollars on the project. Phosphate had been discovered halfway up the Peace River in 1885, and by 1892, it was Tampa's largest export commodity. Port Tampa was booming.

In 1890, Plant completed his first hotel, the forty-room Port Tampa Inn. (Actually, a smaller, seven-room annex to the hotel was completed and opened a year earlier.) It was three stories tall and built out over the water on pilings halfway out to the end of the dock. Before it opened, construction had already begun on one of Plant's most beautiful projects, the Tampa Bay Hotel. In the meantime, he also bought the existing 150-room Seminole Hotel in Winter Park.

Henry Plant agreed to build the Tampa Bay Hotel along the banks of the Hillsborough River if the town of Tampa would construct a bridge over the river to give easy access to the Hillsborough County Courthouse on the opposite side. The town built the bridge and also offered property tax incentives. Plant hired architect John A. Wood, who had designed hotels in New York and in Georgia, to design his hotel. It would be an exotic, four-story brick structure topped with six towering, Moorish minarets. The interior was just as elegant, with horseshoe-arched throughways and windows and a wide, winding mahogany staircase in the lobby. A two-story verandah with elaborate lace brackets in its roof supports surrounded the exterior. The Tampa Bay Hotel, which opened on February 5, 1891, featured a dining hall, a café, a drug and sundries shop, a barbershop, even a billiards room. Guests never needed to leave the premises. Plant insisted that his hotel rival Henry Flagler's Ponce De Leon Hotel in St. Augustine, which had opened in 1888. Plant's hotel did fairly well in its first years but never really met his expectations as a resort for the ultra-wealthy. Flagler had beat him to the punch.

Perhaps the Tampa Bay Hotel reached its peak in 1898, during the Spanish-American War, when troops (including Teddy Roosevelt and his Rough Riders) amassed in Tampa for embarkation to Cuba. It would remain a hotel until 1930. In 1933, it became the University of Tampa, which it still is today.

During the 1890s, Plant acquired or built six more hotels—in Ocala, Kissimmee, Punta Gorda, Ft. Myers, Palm Harbor, and Clearwater, where he built the magnificent Belleview Biltmore (see Clearwater chapter, Belleview Biltmore Resort & Spa).

Henry Plant died on June 23, 1899. He was eighty. At that time his various companies employed thirteen thousand people in railroad lines, steamship lines, real estate companies, and hotels.

I find the similarity in these two men's lives remarkable. They had similar drive, rose up from similar meager backgrounds, took similar risks, and suffered similar losses. Ultimately, both were enormously influential in the development of Florida, perhaps more so than anyone else in the state's history. The two men were acquainted with each other. Along the way, some minor business was transacted between them, or at least between their respective companies. Mostly they were congenial rivals. Though it's never been proven, some speculate that the two men had a gentlemen's agreement never to invade each other's coast.

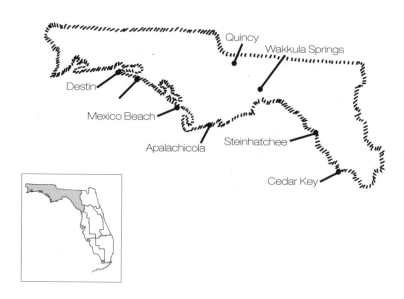

Quincy

Wakkula Springs

Destin

Mexico Beach

Apalachicola

Steinhatchee

Cedar Key

NORTHWEST

Gazebo at the Driftwood Inn,
Mexico Beach

Destin

Henderson Park Inn
2700 Highway 98 East
Destin, Florida 32541
(850) 837-4853
(800) 336-4853
innkeeper@hendersonparkinn.com
www.hendersonparkinn.com

35 rooms, $94–318
restaurant, beachfront, pool

THEY CAN CALL IT the "Redneck Riviera" if they want to, but Florida's Panhandle beaches are the widest and whitest. Panhandle beach sand is a sparkling white, powdered quartz, washed down from the Appalachian Mountains over the eons. It's so fine it squeaks when you walk on it.

Destin's Henderson Park Inn may be the best place to stay if you want to be right on that beach. It resembles an old Cape Cod mansion, with shake shingle sides, steep green roof, and wide curving verandah, but it was just built in 1992. It's actually two three-story buildings. There are twenty rooms in one, fifteen in the other. Most of the rooms have Jacuzzi tubs, refrigerators, and microwaves. All are furnished with reproduction Victorian antique furniture, and all have private balconies or porches that overlook the emerald green Gulf of Mexico. No need to drive into town for a meal—the Verandah restaurant offers fresh seafood, served inside or out on the porch.

What makes the Henderson Park Inn's location so perfect is that the property borders one of the prettiest beach parks in the state, Henderson Beach State Park. Unlike the rest of the state, in the Panhandle winter is the low season and summer is the high season. I like it in late fall and winter. Besides the fact that everything is less expensive, the weather is perfect (except for an occasional hurricane) and you can walk for an hour down the beach without seeing another person.

Seaside

HALFWAY BETWEEN PANAMA CITY and Fort Walton Beach, Walton County Road 30A detours off of the main thoroughfare, Highway 98. It winds down to the shoreline and the quaint beachside communities of Seagrove, Grayton Beach, and Seaside. Both the highway and the homes along the road sit atop a coastal bluff that drops off to gorgeous beaches on the Gulf of Mexico. Sea oats and wind-stunted scrub oaks sprout from the sand dunes.

Robert Davis spent his childhood summers in the 1950s at Seagrove, just down the beach from a large plot of undeveloped land that his grandfather owned. When Davis inherited the property in 1978, he decided to build a small beach community that would echo those childhood summer memories. The result was Seaside, an eighty-acre town of wood-framed, tin-roofed, screen-porched Florida beach cottages in every color the folks at Crayola ever imagined.

Seaside is a walking town with brick streets and sand-and-shell pathways. A leisurely walk from one end of town to the other takes less than half an hour. Seaside's focal point, the town square, has an amphitheater, restaurants, shops, galleries, and a terrific gourmet market called the Modica. Across CR 30A from the square on the beach side, there are more restaurants and boutiques. There is no mowable grass except in the center of the town square—only native scrub oaks, shrubs, loblolly pines, and palm trees. All of

Natchez Street Beach
Pavilion at Seaside

the cottages and houses are built in a similar Florida beach bungalow style architecture, but no two are even remotely alike. There are surprises around every corner. White picket fences (a code requirement) of all different styles front each home, and gingerbread details on the porches and windows add whimsical character. This is a hammocks-and-rocking-chairs kind of place.

On the beach side, seven distinct and architecturally dramatic open-air pavilions with boardwalks invite residents across the dunes and down onto the beach. Amazingly, Seaside's very restrictive building and architectural code actually seems to open the door to diversity, individuality, and imagination.

Davis went to architects Andres Duany and Elizabeth Plater-Zyberk at Arquitectonica in Miami to help plan the layout of Seaside and to draw up the town's building codes. Seaside's first houses went up in 1982. Since then, the architectural world has praised it as a community that blends function, beauty, and a definitive sense of place like no other. It is one of the original New Urbanism towns. Sometimes called Neo-traditional Town Planning or Traditional Neighborhood Design, New Urbanism is a community design concept that attempts to maximize the interaction of neighbors, to minimize automobile use, and to place a town's (or neighborhood's) living quarters within walking distance of its commercial center. "New" is somewhat of a misnomer. The concept is based largely on old ideas and a return to pre–World War II (read: pre–suburban sprawl) style neighborhoods and towns.

Most of the cottages in Seaside can be rented through the Seaside Cottage Rental Agency. Also, Bud and Alley's Restaurant, on the beach side of County Road 30A, is superb!

Josephine's French Country Inn
P.O. Box 4767
Seaside, Florida 32459
(800) 848-1840
(850) 231-1939
(850) 231-2446 fax

11 accommodations (7 rooms and 4 suites), $130–220
full breakfast, non-smoking, full kitchens in the suites, bicycles,
handicap-accessible room, gourmet restaurant also serves dinner

JOSEPHINE'S FRENCH COUNTRY INN is Seaside's only bed & breakfast. At first glance it appears somewhat formal among the cottages. Its six towering columns and full-width double-porch facade resemble Greek Revival architecture more than beach bungalow. Four-poster beds, antiques, beautiful mahogany interior trim, and an outstanding French country restaurant make this an elegant inn. But don't worry. The attitude at Josephine's is still all "beach," and they won't fret if you track a little sand through the front door.

There are seven rooms in the main inn and four suites adjacent to it. The third-floor cupola has one of the best 360-degree views in Seaside.

Seaside Cottage Rental Agency
P.O. Box 4730
Seaside, Florida 32459
(800) 277-8696
(850) 231-1320

Bud and Alley's Restaurant
Cinderella Circle
CR 30A
Seaside, Florida 32459
(850) 231-5900

Mexico Beach

MEXICO BEACH IS THE FIRST real mainland beach you come to when you travel west on Highway 98 into the Panhandle. Houses sit high up on a bluff and look across the highway, over sea oats, to the beach and the Gulf. Mexico Beach was developed in the 1950s and still retains a bit of the beach-town flavor from that era.

Driftwood Inn
2105 Highway 98
P.O. Box 13447
Mexico Beach, Florida 32410
(850) 648-5126
peggy@driftwoodinn.com
www.driftwoodinn.com

18 main inn rooms, $95–115
6 units in duplex cottages, $95–105
4 Victorian houses, $140–150
Continental breakfast, pool, beachside, wedding chapel on premises

Driftwood Inn

THE DRIFTWOOD INN, at Mexico Beach's west end, is a quaint beach hotel. The original inn was built in the early 1950s. Tom and Peggy Wood bought it in 1975. After a fire destroyed the main building in 1994, the Woods decided to rebuild in an architectural style that mirrored the original. The lobby doubles as an antiques store, and the bright red tin roof and white decorative railings remind me of Seaside. Recently, they've added some separate single and duplex bungalows. Antique furniture, wood floors, and raised ceilings in some units add to the Driftwood's beach-Victorian atmosphere.

The Woods also own four Victorian-style houses across the road from the main inn. And for guests who want a beach wedding, the Woods have built their very own beachside wedding chapel.

Apalachicola

APALACHICOLA, FLORIDA'S FAMOUS OYSTER capital, sits on the end of the elbow in the Panhandle, where the Apalachicola River joins the Gulf of Mexico. Its history has seesawed between booms and economic droughts. In the 1820s, it was a big cotton shipping port. Cotton warehouses went up along the river in 1838, and in 1839, Florida's first railroad opened from here to St. Joseph (now Port St. Joe) to the west. That railroad didn't last, though. An outbreak of yellow fever decimated St. Joseph in 1841. In 1844, it was flooded by a hurricane. Twenty years later, new railroads rerouted trade east and west, and for a while Apalachicola lost its importance as a port. But in the 1880s, cypress milling revitalized the town. Then in the 1920s, it became the center of Florida's booming seafood industry. Apalachicola is, to this day, best known for its oysters.

Currently, another kind of revitalization is taking place in Apalachicola. Preservation of the town's heritage and its century-old Victorian houses is taking the spotlight. Much of the downtown and dock area has also been restored. Some good restaurants have opened. The Owl Café/That Place in Apalach is one of the best.

The Gibson Inn
57 Market Street
Apalachicola, Florida 32320
(850) 653-2191
(850) 653-3521
www.gibsoninn.com

31 rooms $75–125
restaurant, bar

THE GIBSON INN IS the centerpiece of Apalachicola's historic district. It was the Franklin Inn when James Fulton Buck opened it in 1907. The name changed in 1923, when the Gibson sisters bought it. These were grand years at the inn, but the opulence of that era declined with the passing decades. The Gibson Inn had been boarded up for some time when, in 1983, Michael Koun, his brother, Neal, and some investing friends bought the hotel for $90,000. Over the next two years, they spent $1 million, meticulously rebuilding and restoring it to its original turn-of-the-century grandeur. Their best architectural reference was a collection of old photos taken in 1910. The

The Gibson Inn

photographer had spent that year photographing Apalachicola and the surrounding area. Now, a number of those pictures hang on the walls in the inn's dining room.

When the National Trust for Historic Preservation published its coffee-table book, *America Restored* (Preservation Press, 1994), the Gibson Inn was one oftwo Florida buildings featured. Blue and gray with white trim, the three-story Victorian-style hotel is the first thing you see after crossing the Apalachicola River. A widow's walk crowns its tin roof. Wide first- and second-floor verandahs wrap around three of its sides. Wooden rockers and Adirondack chairs on the verandahs invite the inn's guests to "set a spell," have a cup of coffee, read a book, or maybe just scratch behind the ears of one of the four resident cats.

Four-poster beds and other period antiques decorate each of the Gibson Inn's thirty-one guest rooms. Wooden slat blinds shade the windows. Artisans built the lobby staircase from scratch, using a single surviving newel post as their guide. Rich cypress woodwork can be found throughout the inn. My favorite room, the bar, has a grand nautical feel about it; it would have been at home on the *Titanic*. Just two weeks after the Gibson reopened, in November 1985, Hurricane Kate slammed the central Panhandle. The Kouns kept the bar open and threw a Key Largo–style hurricane party. Humphrey Bogart would have approved.

For breakfast one morning at the restaurant, I had their exceptional French toast, made with two-inch-thick slices of the inn's freshly baked bread. The dinner menu is tempting too. Their New Orleans chef prepares entrees like Grouper Papillote and Oysters Remick.

Coombs House Inn

80 Sixth Street
Apalachicola, Florida 32320
(850) 653-9199
(850) 653-2785
coombsstaff@coomb shouseinn.com
www.coombshouseinn.com

18 rooms $79–175
full breakfast, non-smoking, bicycles (one tandem),
beach chairs and umbrellas

Coombs
House Inn

WHEN AN INTERNATIONALLY RENOWNED interior decorator buys a bed & breakfast, you might expect to see something beyond the ordinary. Such is the case with the Coombs House Inn, and I guarantee it exceeds any expectations you might have. Decorator Lynn Wilson bought it in 1992. It had been condemned and was in danger of being torn down when Lynn rescued it. She spent two years rebuilding and restoring it and turning it into an elegant Victorian showcase.

James Coombs, a wealthy Apalachicola lumber baron, built the house in 1905. He constructed much of the interior from rich black cypress (the source of Coombs' wealth), including the paneled walls in the foyer, the floors, the massive ceiling trusses, and most notably the grand and intricately carved staircase.

There are nine rooms in the original Coombs house. Lynn recently added a second house (which she also restored extensively), the Dr. Marks House, one block east. Locals call it the Annex. It adds nine rooms, including a room in the carriage house. The inn offers something else rarely found but often looked for—Camillia Hall, a separate reception room with a large garden yard and a gazebo for weddings and other special events.

The Owl Café/That Place in Apalach
15 Avenue D
Apalachicola, Florida 32320
(850) 653-9888

Quincy

THE TOWN OF QUINCY, in the center of north Florida's Panhandle, traces its heritage to and derives much of its character from the Deep South. It's the Gadsden County seat. Like so many small towns in Georgia and Alabama, it has a stately, dome-topped courthouse, with four massive white columns, in the middle of the town square. A Civil War monument on the south side of the courthouse reads, "Sacred to the memory of the Confederate soldiers from ante-bellum Gadsden County, Florida, who died in the defense of their country."

Quincy's entire downtown and the surrounding neighborhood are listed as a historic district on the National Register of Historic Places. The residential neighborhood has quite a few restored post- and antebellum mansions, a couple of which are now bed & breakfasts.

There is an interesting historical side note that connects Quincy with the

McFarlin House

Coca-Cola Company. In the early 1900s, patrons of the Quincy State Bank (Florida's first chartered state bank) were told that purchasing stock in a fledgling drink company might prove to be a good investment. Lots of Quincyites took that advice and became wealthy. For many years, residents in Quincy held more than half of Coca-Cola's outstanding shares. Today they are still thought to own as much as ten percent of Coca-Cola's stock.

McFarlin House Bed & Breakfast

305 East King Street
Quincy, Florida 32351
(850) 875-2526
inquiries@mcfarlinhouse.com
www.mcfarlinhouse.com

9 rooms, $65–175
full breakfast, handicap access, non-smoking inside

TOBACCO FARMER AND LUMBER baron John Lee McFarlin built the three-story McFarlin House, an exquisite example of Queen Anne Victorian architecture, in 1895. Richard and Tina Fauble purchased it in 1994 and performed a complete restoration before opening the McFarlin House Bed & Breakfast in 1995. The Faubles were not novices in restoration work. They had restored several properties before buying this house, and their expertise is evident.

McFarlin House features an octagonal turret, beveled and stained-glass windows, a double front door with leaded-glass windows, curly pine paneling, stamped copper ceilings, Italian tile, and seven fireplaces with French hand-carved mantles. Double-grouped columns support the roof over a wide, three-sided verandah that curves gracefully around the corners of the house.

The second-floor King's View Room, which overlooks King Street, has a two-person whirlpool tub surrounded on three sides by seven windows. Its queen-size bed sits in the expanded corner created by the second story of the turret. The Pink Magnolia Room occupies the third story of the turret.

The Allison House Inn
215 North Madison Street
Quincy, Florida 32351
(850) 875-2511 voice and fax
(888) 904-2511
innkeeper@tds.net
www.travelguides.com/home/allison_house

5 rooms, $75–90
Continental breakfast, non-smoking, small pets welcome,
 handicap access

ABRAHAM K. ALLISON WAS president of the Florida Senate in 1865, when Governor John Milton committed suicide to avoid capture by Union troops during the last days of the Civil War. Allison was next in line to take over as governor, and Union authorities promptly jailed him for six months. After his incarceration, he returned to Quincy to practice law.

Allison built his family's piling-elevated, Georgian Colonial house in 1843. They remained there until 1893, when Allison died. In 1925, the bottom of the house was enclosed around the support pilings to create an additional floor, and the

The Allison House

exterior was re-styled to accommodate the change. The house underwent restoration in 1989 and opened as a bed & breakfast the following year. The interior decor gives the inn a British feel.

Wakulla Springs

WAKULLA SPRINGS IS THE largest and deepest spring in the world. Its waters are so clear that details at the bottom, 185 feet down, are easily discernible from the surface. Universal Studios chose Wakulla Springs as the filming location for their 1954 sci-fi/horror classic *The Creature from the Black Lagoon* because of its exceptionally clear waters. It has also been the site of numerous archaeological excavations. Divers discovered a complete mastodon skeleton at the bottom of the spring in 1935. The mastodon now stands, reconstructed, in the Museum of Florida History in the R. A. Gray Building at the capitol in Tallahassee.

The spring had its own recently living prehistoric creature too, although by all accounts not a malevolent one. Old Joe was a 650-pound, eleven-foot-two-inch-long alligator that had been sighted at the spring since the 1920s. Although he had never shown aggressive behavior, in August 1966, an unknown assailant shot and killed Old Joe. Old Joe's estimated age was two hundred years. Carl Buchheister, then-president of the Audubon Society, offered a $5,000 reward for information leading to the arrest of the killer, but he or she was never found.

All manner of wildlife thrives in the park. In addition to gators, deer, raccoons, and even a few bears live here. Birdwatchers can spot a variety, including anhingas, purple gallinules, herons, egrets, ospreys, and long-billed limpkins (called "crying birds" because of their shrieking, almost humanlike cry).

Wakulla Springs Lodge
Edward Ball/Wakulla Springs State Park
550 Wakulla Park Drive
Wakulla Springs, Florida 32305
(850) 224-5950
(850) 561-7251 fax

27 rooms, $69–90
restaurant, soda fountain shop, non-smoking

EDWARD BALL WAS THE brother-in-law of Alfred I. DuPont. He was also the executor and trustee of DuPont's sizable estate and trust. Ball built a banking, telephone, railroad, and paper and box manufacturing empire out of the DuPont trust, which was worth an estimated $33 million in 1935 when DuPont died. Ball had grown that fortune into more than $2 billion by the time he passed away in 1981 at age ninety-three.

One of Edward Ball's proudest achievements was the construction of the Wakulla Springs Lodge in 1937. The twenty-seven-room lodge is essentially the same today as it was in the 1930s. Ball insisted that it always continue to reflect that era and also that it never become so exclusive it would not be affordable to "common folks."

I visited the lodge and spring on a sunny, fall morning. Wakulla Springs Lodge reminds me of a palatial Spanish hacienda. The first things that caught my eye, when I walked into the lobby, were the cypress ceiling beams with Aztec-style, hand-painted designs on them. Blue and gold Spanish tiles frame the entranceway. The floors are mauve and gray Tennessee marble tiles in a checkerboard pattern. A giant fireplace, made from native limestone and trimmed in marble, dominates the far wall.

A long glass case at one end of the lobby contains the stuffed and mounted remains of Old Joe. His plaque reads, "Old Joe's first and only cage." The most interesting room in the lodge, the soda fountain shop, is just past Old Joe's

Wakulla Springs Lodge

case. There is no bar in the Wakulla Springs Lodge. Instead, Ball, who was fond of ginger whips (ice cream, ginger ale, and whipped cream), had a sixty-foot-long, solid marble soda fountain counter installed.

The lodge and grounds sit on the north bank of the spring. From the top of a twenty-foot-high diving platform, I looked down on bream and bass schooling at the bottom of the spring. The water is amazingly clear and looks like a giant sheet of glass. It's no wonder that Hollywood came to this location to film *Tarzan* features and movies like *Around the World under the Sea, Airport 77*, and *The Creature from the Black Lagoon*.

Steinhatchee

Steinhatchee Landing Resort

P.O. Box 789
Highway 51 North
Steinhatchee, Florida 32359
(800) 584-1709
SLI@Dixie.4ez.com
www.steinhatcheelanding.com

21 accommodations (houses, cottages, townhouses), $120–350 children welcome, small dogs allowed in some units, kitchens and washer/dryer in all units, 11 non-smoking units, sunset pontoon boat cruises, pool, spa, petting zoo, carriage rides, jogging trails, tennis courts, canoes, bicycles, guided fishing trip arrangements

WANDER THE TWO-LANE back roads of Florida's Big Bend region and eventually you'll come across the quiet village of Steinhatchee at the mouth of the Steinhatchee River. Fishing in the river and fishing or scalloping on the grass flats at its mouth (called Deadman's Bay) and out in the Gulf are the primary pastimes here.

Three miles upriver, the Steinhatchee Landing Resort, a nature-conscious village with old Florida–style homes and live oak– and magnolia-shaded lanes, wraps around a bend on the north bank of the Steinhatchee River.

My accommodation for a weekend at Steinhatchee Landing was a quaint, two-story, tin-roofed house. All the houses on this lane are named for spices. Mine was the Vanilla, but it was anything but plain. It's furnished with comfortable, overstuffed chairs and couches. There's a fluffy quilt on the queen-size bed downstairs. The kitchen and a cozy living room, with a vaulted ceiling and windows on three sides, are upstairs. There are also two screened porches, one upstairs and one downstairs, furnished with wicker rocking chairs. This is old, Florida Cracker–style architecture but new construction with all the modern conveniences. From the upstairs porch, I looked out over the Landing's quarter-acre vegetable garden, where green beans, onions, potatoes, tomatoes, and corn are grown for the Steinhatchee Landing Restaurant, which is highly rated and managed by an award-winning gourmet chef.

Developers Dean and Loretta Fowler, originally from Georgia, began building this village in 1990. It has since grown from twenty-five to thirty-five acres. Dean first came down to Taylor County, Florida, in the late 1980s for a weekend fishing expedition at the invitation of a group of banker friends.

In his gentle Georgia accent, Dean told me, "I fell in love with the Steinhatchee River and this rustic fishing village town and decided to build a vacation home here. Before long, Loretta and I were spending the majority of our spare time here. It occurred to me that it was mostly Georgia men that would come here to fish. They rarely brought their families because there wasn't much for families to do. I started thinking about what would families enjoy doing here? Then I started a scratch-pad list that evolved into the idea of a resort complex with the right amenities to attract families."

Dean had built nursing homes and retirement developments in Georgia, so he knew what a project like this entailed.

"Condominium cracker boxes just wouldn't look right in this rustic little town," Dean explained, "so I called the University of Florida School of Architecture to see if they had an expert in vintage Florida architecture. They introduced me to Professor Ron Haase, who had written a book called *Classic Cracker, Florida's Wood Frame Architecture* (Pineapple Press, 1992). Ron came up with the design criteria. He designed the first nine houses and the restaurant. Other architects have designed houses built here, but they follow the guidelines laid out by Ron."

Twenty-one homes have already been built, and there are more on the drawing board. Most are privately owned and rented through the Steinhatchee Landing office. The Fowlers have built a dock on the river that incorporates a resurrected, sixty-year-old wooden bait store and boathouse that was half collapsed and falling in the water when the Fowlers bought this property. They have also built a horse stable (they offer carriage rides), a swimming pool and spa, a covered pavilion with gas grill adjacent to the pool, a children's playground, jogging trails, tennis courts, and a recent addition—a children's petting zoo with goats, chickens, and ducks. They have canoes for exploring the river and will make arrangements for guided fishing. If you don't

Steinhatchee
Landing Resort

feel like paddling or casting, you might like a sunset cruise on Steinhatchee Landing's pontoon boat.

This is a place that welcomes and caters to families. Former president Jimmy Carter, a friend of Dean and Loretta's, brought his entire family, including children and grandchildren, here for their Christmas family gathering. Reportedly, Mrs. Carter outfished her husband.

When Dean first began to clear the Steinhatchee Landing property, he came across something unexpected. "I found some interesting artifacts, most of them in that small creek that runs through the property," Dean said while pointing out one of the office windows. He picked up a smoky glass bottle and handed it to me. The imperfect shape and the bubbles in the glass indicated that it was old. "I found a lot of bottles, most broken but some intact like this one, probably a wine bottle. A bottle expert told me that this one dates back to the 1840s." I very carefully handed it back.

He continued, "Here's something else that I found in the creek." He lifted a wooden stake with a forged iron clasp around one end. "We think this might have been a tent pole. The creek yielded quite a bit of old, square-cut lumber in addition to the bottle pieces. Also, we found a still-intact and upright railing for tying horses up to."

In 1838, during the height of the Second Seminole War, General Zachary Taylor ordered the building of Fort Frank Brooke on the banks of the Steinhatchee River. There is convincing historical evidence that it was built very near, or possibly right on, the land that Steinhatchee Landing occupies. In a Gulf Coast Historical Review article, historian Niles Schuh points out that army personnel reports and letters from those who operated in this area during the Second Seminole War record that "the falls of Steinhatchee River are six miles above Fort Frank Brooke." If their mileage estimates were accurate, this description places the fort at the same bend in the river where Steinhatchee Landing is now. From the bottom of the river at the bend, scuba divers frequently bring up artifacts like utensils and buttons from military jackets. Maps from that time, although not detailed, show the fort at a bend in the river in approximately the same location.

Michael and Leslie Poole, very dear friends from my high school days, told me about Steinhatchee Landing. They and their two sons, Blake and Preston, have been coming here on an annual weekend fishing trip since the boys were old enough to bait their own hooks. The Pooles are like many of Dean and Loretta's guests, who make a standing reservation for the same time each year.

Steinhatchee Landing is such a serene place that it's tempting to make a permanent reservation every year for the entire year.

Cedar Key

CEDAR KEY TODAY LOOKS a lot like Key West of forty years ago. It has that special eclectic feel that remote island communities seem to acquire. The whiff of salt and fish is always in the air. No one is in a hurry. Except during festival weekends, this is a quiet place—much quieter than it was over a century ago.

In the 1870s and 1880s, Cedar Key experienced its cedar lumber industry boom. Lumber mills on adjacent keys milled cedar for making pencils. A. W. Faber had a mill on Atsena Otie Key, half a mile offshore. Fishing and lumber shipping were also important businesses in Cedar Key. For awhile, this was Florida's most strategic port. Florida's first cross-state railroad, the Atlantic to Gulf/Florida Railroad Company Line, completed in 1861, ran from Fernandina to Cedar Key.

Cedar Key has a history of attracting famous writers and visionaries. John

D. McDonald wrote some of his Travis McGee books here and occasionally used Cedar Key as a setting for his novels. John Muir concluded his one-thousand-mile walk from Indiana to the Gulf of Mexico in 1867 and remained in Cedar Key for several months to study the eco-structure of the coast.

Second Street, located downtown, and Dock Street, built out over the water, are Cedar Key's two main streets. Galleries, seafood eateries, and craft shops make up most of the businesses. There are also two historical museums. Two annual festivals bring visitors from around the state. The Seafood Festival is in October, and the Sidewalk Arts and Crafts Festival is in April.

Island Hotel and Restaurant

373 2nd Street
Cedar Key, Florida 32625
(352) 543-5111
(800) 432-4640
(352) 543-6949 fax
info@islandhotel-cedarkey.com
reservations@islandhotel-cedarkey.com
www.islandhotel-cedarkey.com

13 rooms (11 with private baths, 2 with shared baths), $65–125 non-smoking inside except for the Neptune Bar, full breakfast included,
limited suitability for children (no children permitted on holiday or festival weekends)

CEDAR KEY'S MOST FAMOUS landmark, The Island Hotel, has survived ravaging hurricanes, floods, fires, and the Civil War. It was constructed with oak beam frames, hand-cut wooden floors and interior walls, and twelve-inch-

Island Hotel

thick, oyster-shell-reinforced tabby exterior walls. From the outside, the hotel appears unchanged from eighty-year-old photos of it at the Cedar Key Historical Society Museum.

It was built in 1859 as Parsons and Hale's General Store. When Union troops invaded the town during the Civil War, they burned most of the buildings but left the store standing because they needed it to warehouse supplies and house their troops. No doubt this was a frustrating time for owner Maj. John Parsons, who commanded a detachment of Confederate volunteers.

Following the war, Parsons and his partner, Francis Hale, reopened the general store. Famous naturalist John Muir described the store in his journal in 1867: "I stepped into a little store, which had a considerable trade in quinine, and alligator and rattlesnake skins. . . ." Sometime in the 1880s, Parsons and Hale began taking boarders and serving meals. In 1896, before hurricanes were assigned names, a furious hurricane hit Cedar Key, devastating most of it but leaving the store intact. Most people mark the 1896 hurricane as the end of Cedar Key's prosperous industrial period.

Simon Feinberg, a property investor, bought the building in 1859 and remodeled it into the Bay Hotel. The downstairs and second-floor verandahs, which wrap around two sides of the hotel, were added during his tenure. In the years that followed, the hotel changed names and owners frequently. During the Depression, one owner tried to burn it down three times, but the fire department was just across the street and always managed to save it.

Everyone seems to agree that the hotel's heyday began in 1946, when Bessie and Loyal Gibbs bought it and renamed it the Island Hotel. Prior owners had, over the last decade or so, operated a brothel out of the place, and it had become quite rundown. Bessie and Loyal toiled exhaustively to put the hotel back into shape. Gibby ran the bar and Bessie ran the restaurant. In 1948, they hired artist Helen Tooker to paint the picture of King Neptune that still hangs up behind the bar today. That painting, like the hotel, seems to be blessed with multiple lives. It has survived gunshots and hurricanes—even flooding when a 1950 hurricane tore part of the Island Hotel's roof off. Bessie's culinary skills, restaurant-operating talents, and panache with the clientele won the Gibbses fame and customers. Loyal died in 1962, and Bessie, while still owning and operating the hotel, went on to become Cedar Key's mayor from 1967 to 1968. She started the very popular Annual Arts and Crafts Festival, and she was instrumental in getting the Cedar Key Museum open. With her health deteriorating, she sold the Island Hotel in 1974 and died the following year.

Over the decades, the Island Hotel has been host to Florida politicians; famous writers, such as Pearl Buck and John D. McDonald; actresses and actors; and singers, such as Tennessee Ernie Ford and, more recently, Jimmy

Buffet, who would sometimes perform impromptu in the Neptune Bar in the 1970s.

Like the island of Cedar Key, the Island Hotel is rustic, with weathered wood and cracked plaster on its exterior, but that's all integral to its slice-of-Florida's-past charm. The restaurant is still famous for its native Florida seafood dishes, like soft-shell blue crab, and its hearts-of-palm salad—Bessie's recipe.

Cedar Key Bed & Breakfast

Cedar Key Bed & Breakfast
810 Third Street
Cedar Key, Florida 32625
(352) 543-9000
(877) 543-5051
(352) 543-8070

bob@cedarkeybedbreakfast.com
www.cedarkeybedbreakfast.com

6 rooms, 1 cottage, $75–120
full breakfast, non-smoking, inquire
about lodgings for young children

ONLY A THREE-BLOCK stroll from downtown Cedar Key and two blocks from the Gulf, the Cedar Key Bed & Breakfast occupies the tin-roofed, two-story, historic Wadley House. The Eagle Cedar Mill Company built it as an employee residence in 1880, at the height of Cedar Key's cedar industry boom. For a while, the daughter of David Yulee, Florida's first U. S. senator, who also built the Atlantic to Gulf/Florida Railroad, operated a boarding house out of it. In 1919, B. C. Wadley purchased it, and it remained with his family until 1991.

Richard and Brenda Pancake restored it and converted it into a bed & breakfast in 1991–1992. Current owners Lois Benninghoff and Bob Davenport bought it in 1994 and expanded it by adding on to the house and cultivating a spacious garden adjacent to it. Six rooms are in the main house, and the one-room Honeymoon Cottage attaches to the porch at the rear and has its own private entrance.

Amelia Island

St. Augustine
St. Augustine Beach

High Springs
Gainesville
Micanopy

NORTHEAST

BRUCE HUNT

Magnolia Plantation, Gainesville

Amelia Island

Fernandina/Amelia Island History

FLORIDA'S TOWNS WITH THE richest histories, like St. Augustine and Key West, also seem to have the best selection of bed & breakfasts. This is certainly true for Fernandina Beach, on Amelia Island north of Jacksonville. Eight flags have flown over Amelia Island (more than any other location in the United States). Primarily it has been occupied by Spain, France, the United States, and Great Britain. It was British General James Oglethorpe who named the island Amelia after the daughter of King George II. Others occupied it for transient periods. In 1812, a small group of U. S. patriots who called themselves the Patriots of Amelia Island overthrew the Spanish on the island and raised their own flag for a very brief time. In the summer of 1817, Sir Gregor MacGregor seized control of Spain's recently completed island fortification, Fort San Carlos. MacGregor flew his Green Cross flag but withdrew a short time later. A few months after that, French pirate Luis Aury raided the island and raised the Mexican flag—without Mexico's authorization. In April 1861, Confederate troops occupied Fort Clinch at the north end of the island, but Federal troops regained it a year later.

It was the railroad that turned Fernandina into a thriving place in the mid to late nineteenth century. Originally the town was located about three quarters of a mile north of its present location. In the 1850s, railroad owner and Florida's first senator, David Yulee, promised its residents prosperity if they would agree to move the community south—to better accommodate his railroad terminus and port on the Amelia River. They agreed, and Fernandina's Golden Era began. In a short time, luxury steamers from the North began bringing wealthy vacationers to Amelia Island. Luxury hotels were constructed, both in town and on the beach. Palatial Victorian mansions went up on the streets north and south of Centre Street. Fernandina's naturally deep harbor allowed large ships into its port. The lumber, cotton, turpentine, phosphate, and naval stores shipping and rail transport industries boomed. The Spanish-American War in 1898 generated even more shipping and rail business. Not only did Yulee's promise hold up, it exceeded everyone's expectations. For nearly fifty years, the new Fernandina was both a world-renowned resort and a center of commerce.

It was during this time that Standard Oil mogul and railroad tycoon Henry Flagler set his sights on Florida. In the 1880s, he had begun building resort hotels along Florida's east coast. As the hotels were completed, he would

BRUCE HUNT

Elizabeth Pointe Lodge,
Amelia Island

string them together with his railroad. Flagler bypassed Amelia Island, choosing not to connect with Yulee's railroad line. As a result, by the early 1900s Fernandina's tourist trade had moved south to St. Augustine (Flagler's Ponce de Leon Hotel) and to Palm Beach (Flagler's Royal Poinciana and Breakers Hotels). Fernandina's flourish fizzled almost as rapidly as it had begun. In the long run, this may have been a blessing in disguise. Had Flagler chosen instead to bring his rail line through Fernandina, Amelia Island may well have turned into a Manhattan Island South. The Victorian homes and Centre Street's brick buildings would no doubt have been replaced with larger and more modern structures. In a very roundabout way, we can probably thank Henry Flagler for saving the Fernandina Beach that we know today.

Fernandina's Centre Street Historic District is one of the best renovations I've seen. Interesting galleries, shops, and excellent restaurants (the Beech Street Grille is my favorite) are plentiful.

The Fairbanks House

227 South Street
Fernandina Beach, Florida 32034
(904) 277-0500
(800) 261-4838
fairbanks@net-magic.net
www.fairbankshouse.com

12 rooms, $150–250
full breakfast, bicycles, beach chairs, non-smoking
(including grounds), no children

BILL AND THERESA HAMILTON spent ten years kicking the "owning a bed and breakfast" idea around. They like to travel, and they had stayed in a lot of inns and bed & breakfasts. With each passing year, they became a little more knowledgeable and a little more serious about the endeavor. Theresa tells me, "We considered New Orleans, and we looked very closely at Savannah."

Bill adds, "Our criteria were that the location had to have a year-round warm climate, be near water, and be in an urban area where guests could walk to shops and restaurants. That pretty much confined our zone to the southeast Atlantic coast and some spots along the Gulf coast."

The Hamiltons used a consultant to help them find and procure their property. "It's not buying a house. It's buying a business," Theresa says. "Owning and operating a bed & breakfast is a full-time, seven-days-a-week job. There is so much that goes on behind the scenes in order to make the guest's experience what it should be."

Prior to purchasing the Fairbanks House, Theresa had been in computer sales and had also owned her own business for a while, both experiences she has found useful in running a bed & breakfast. Bill was a project manager for a building construction firm—definitely useful background for the bed & breakfast business.

"In this business," Theresa explains, "life is a whole lot easier if you are knowledgeable about building maintenance, plumbing, electrical—and if you are capable of doing that type of work yourself. I always tell Bill that even if I wasn't married to him, I'd ask him to go into business with me."

The Fairbanks House was not for sale when the Hamiltons found it. They point out that the advantage of looking at properties that aren't currently for sale is that you're more apt to be looking at ones that are in tip-top shape. Nelson and Mary Smelker had owned and operated it for about three years (it had been rented out as apartments prior to that) when Bill and Theresa came along in 1997.

"The Smelkers did an extraordinary job with this place," Theresa declares. "Mary Smelker has an eye that is second to none. She did every bit of the decorating that you see. She made the bedspreads, the window treatments; she reupholstered the furniture with matching fabrics!" The Smelkers also did extensive remodeling and landscaping. They added a swimming pool, a parking area, additional bathrooms (most with Jacuzzi tubs), plus they purchased three adjacent cottages and added them to the inn. Two were original Fairbanks structures—a caretaker's cottage and a servant's quarters. The third was Fernandina's original schoolhouse.

The inn met all of Bill and Theresa's criteria, and it was fully operational. "And we were charmed," adds Theresa, "by both the Fairbanks House and the town of Fernandina, a wonderful place filled with genuinely friendly people. We fell in love with all of it."

The Fairbanks House is a colossal, three-story (four when you include the tower) Italianate estate. Many consider it to be the finest and best-preserved example of Italianate architecture in Florida. It has all of the identifying characteristics of that 1850–1890 style: tall, narrow windows, some with arches; decorative roof eaves and brackets; decorative porch columns; elabo-

rately detailed molding and trim; ornate brick chimneys; and, of course, a tower. There are ten fireplaces. Tiles that depict Shakespearean characters frame the living room fireplace, and the dining room fireplace has Aesop's Fables characters on its tiles. The floors are heart of pine, and the grand staircase is Honduran mahogany.

The inn's grounds take up half the block between Beech and Cedar Streets. There are nine rooms in the main house, including two suites, plus the three cottages, for a

The Fairbanks House

total of twelve rooms. The Tower Suite, which occupies the entire third floor, has two bedrooms, a living room, and a kitchen. A ladder leads up into the fifteen-foot-high, glass-enclosed, air-conditioned tower, which is furnished with an antique French game table and chairs. Of course, the best thing is the view across the rooftops of Fernandina's Victorian neighborhoods that look like something out of Mary Poppins.

Five years before his death, George Fairbanks and his granddaughter watched from that tower the southern horizon light up with the blazes of the 1901 fire that leveled downtown Jacksonville (over forty miles away). Senator David Yulee had lured George Rainsford Fairbanks to Fernandina in 1879 to run the town's Florida Mirror Newspaper. Fairbanks had been a Confederate Civil War major. He was also a historian, an educator, a former state senator, and one of the founders of the University of the South in Sewanee, Tennessee.

Fairbanks built his house in 1885 at the height of Fernandina's "Golden Era." He commissioned the home's design to famous architect Robert Schuyler. It was the town's most extravagant residence. It had indoor plumbing, a telephone, a cistern for collecting rainwater, and a dumbwaiter for lifting firewood from the basement to the upper floors. Yes, the Fairbanks House has a basement, a Florida rarity.

Local lore claims that Fairbanks built the house as a surprise for his wife. But, reportedly, Mrs. Fairbanks was not pleasantly surprised. "Too ostentatious," she was rumored to have proclaimed, and the house became known as "Fairbanks' Folly." Theresa isn't convinced that that's how it really happened."Just look at all the walk-in closets and the bedrooms designed with sitting rooms off to the side. Look at the layout of the kitchen—a woman was involved in the design of this house, and I think it's likely that it was Mrs. Fairbanks. This was the most opulent of quite a few mansions that were being built during that time. My guess is that there might have been some jealousy in the neighborhood when this house was going up. Rumors get started, stories get told—next thing you know it gets labeled 'Fairbanks' Folly'."

Theresa contends—and I strongly agree—that the bed & breakfast industry has been a great thing for historical restoration. "Today most of these beautiful and enormous old historic homes are too big and too maintenance intensive and expensive to be occupied by an individual family. It takes regular income to keep them up." Also, bed & breakfast owners have a keen interest in maintaining the historical integrity of their houses; it attracts their clientele.

I stayed for two nights in #11, which occupies the entire upstairs in the caretaker's cottage (Bill and Theresa live downstairs). It has one bedroom with a king-size bed, a kitchenette, and a roomy bathroom with both a shower and a Jacuzzi tub. A bright green-and-white vine print wallpaper grows up the walls and across the ceiling, which vaults above the bed. A roof skylight lets a shaft of light into the room at daybreak. The other windows overlook the garden. Entry is private since the cottage is separate from the main house, and during my visit I never heard a sound other than the chirping of birds in the trees just outside my windows.

Breakfast at the Fairbanks House is a marvelous treat. On this pleasantly cool, fall morning, we dined on the verandah overlooking the pool. Delicious banana sorbet with kiwifruit puree was the starter. For the main course, they served orange pecan French toast. This is not your garden-variety French toast. The bread soaks overnight in an egg batter with orange juice and nutmeg. Then they top it with chopped pecans, bake it, and drown it in a rich caramel topping. I'm getting hungry just writing about it. Breakfast, like everything else at the Fairbanks, was a luxurious experience and a feast for the senses.

The Bailey House

28 South 7th Street
Fernandina Beach, Florida 32034
(904) 261-5390
(800) 251-5390
bailey@net-magic.net
www.bailey-house.com

10 rooms, $115—175
full breakfast, non-smoking inside, prefer children over 8,
no alcoholic beverages

THE BAILEY HOUSE IS a postcard-perfect example of classic Queen Anne Victorian architecture. Its steep, pitched roof, two octagonal turrets, broad wraparound porch, and prominent third-floor dormer with scallop-shingled gable identify it as such. But it is the decorative detailing that makes this such an outstanding house.

Effingham Bailey was a steamship agent who would arrange for ships to be brought into Fernandina's port, and by all accounts he was a very successful one. He had the house built as a wedding present for his wife, Kate MacDonnel, on property owned by her family. Construction began in 1892 and took three years to complete. Bailey had access to ship's carpenters who were expert at intricate woodworking. Their craftsmanship is evident both inside and outside the house. Surprisingly for a house this large and complex, the construction plans were mail-order. They came from Knoxville, Tennessee,

The Bailey House

architect George Barber. Many of Barber's Victorian houses still stand across the country.

Tom and Jenny Bishop purchased the Bailey House in 1993. It had been a bed & breakfast since 1983 and a private residence prior to that. Descendants of the Bailey family lived in the house until 1963. The Bailey family Bible is on display in the lobby, where guests can see the handwritten notes that trace the family's history back to November 18, 1860.

Although I walked in unannounced, Tom Bishop offered to give me a tour. He told me, "This was a new venture and an adventure for us. It was a four-room bed and breakfast when Jenny and I bought it. In nineteen ninety-seven, we remodeled everything and added five rooms. We're sorting out the plans to add a tenth room right now." (The tenth room is finished as of this writing.)

Some of the remodeling was true restoration. For instance, the Bishops rebuilt, to the house's original specifications, the spacious front and side wrap-around porches, with their detailed scrollwork on the railing and columns. Beautiful stained-glass transom windows in the lobby and at the staircase landing color the light that pours into the entryway. The new five-room addition, on the north side of the house, blends so seamlessly that I can't tell where the old ends and the new begins.

"Right down to the antique light fixtures and doorknobs and quarter-sawn heart pine floors, we did everything we could to make the addition indistinguishable from the original architecture," Tom explained. Eight of the rooms have bay windows or a corner, octagonal sitting area. Authentic Victorian-era furnishings—including claw-foot bathtubs, Oriental rugs, and antique desks, dressers, and armoires—give guests the impression that they have slipped back in time to the late 1800s. The Bishops' collection of antique beds fascinates me. The Victorian Room has a genuine Victorian sleigh bed. Kate's Room has a queen-size mahogany bed—likely to have been made in Germany a century ago—with intricate carving and brass and mother-of-pearl inlays. Both the Queen Anne Room and Rose's Room have gorgeous king-size, hand-carved mahogany beds.

The Bailey House breakfast menu changes daily, although there are some regular staples like granola.

"Jenny oversees the breakfast. She's also the decorator. I am the dishwasher and the official furniture rearranger under Jenny's direction," Tom commented with a smile.

The Bailey House is both elegant and comfortable. "We wanted it to remind people of their grandmother's house," said Tom. It does remind me of my grandmother's house.

Florida House Inn

20 & 22 South Third Street
Fernandina Beach, Florida 32034
(904) 261-3300
(800) 258-3301
www.floridahouse.com
innkeepers@floridahouse.com

11 rooms, $69–169
full breakfast, dinner available, pub, non-smoking, pets allowed
with prior arrangement

THE FLORIDA HOUSE INN is Florida's oldest continuously operating hotel, built in 1857 by Senator David Yulee's Florida Railroad Company, which also built Florida's first cross-state railroad, which ran from Fernandina (started in 1856) to Cedar Key (completed in 1861).

Owners Bob and Karen Warner have meticulously restored the inn and maintain it in its nineteenth-century grandeur. There are eleven rooms (two are suites). Some have fireplaces, and a few have old-fashioned claw-foot bathtubs.

Florida House Inn

My room at the top of the stairs had a four-poster bed and a ceiling fan and was decorated as if it was the master bedroom in the home of an antiques collector. A plate of chocolate fudge sat on my nightstand.

I wondered who may have slept in the room. In the decades following both the railroad's and the hotel's completion, the Florida House Inn was the place to stay. It hosted many dignitaries: President Ulysses S. Grant stayed there. Jose Marti, renowned Cuban patriot during the Spanish-American War, was a frequent visitor, not to mention Carnegies, DuPonts, and Rockefellers.

While contemplating whether to have that fudge immediately or wait until after dinner, I heard a scratching sound at my door. Thinking that maybe some-one had the wrong room, I opened it and a blur of orange fur darted past my leg and under the bed. It was Tatty, the Warners' tabby cat. Tatty did her five-minute inspection of the room, purred her approval to me, then sauntered down the hall. How's that for charming and homey?

Dinner resembles a Walton family Thanksgiving. The dining room has long tables that seat a dozen each, and meals are served "family style." The group at my table engaged in lively conversation while passing huge bowls of Southern, home-cooked food back and forth. I scooped out big spoonfuls of everything that passed by me—creamed corn, black-eyed peas, turnip greens. Next came the entree platters: fried quail, fried chicken, pork chops—I stabbed one of each (well, two of the quail). Cornbread, sweet tea, and chocolate cake with strawberry–cream cheese frosting rounded out the feast.

Comfortable wicker chairs line the Florida House Inn's second-floor verandah, which overlooks Third Street. Eight flags fly from its railing, one for each owner of Amelia Island. It's the perfect place to relax and watch the sun set over Fernandina's Victorian neighborhood.

Elizabeth Pointe Lodge
98 South Fletcher Avenue
Amelia Island, Florida 32034
(904) 277-4851
(904) 277-6500 fax
(800) 772-3359
inquiries@elizabethpointelodge.com
www.elizabethpointelodge.com

26 rooms, $145–270
full breakfast, light lunch and dinner available, non-smoking inside, beachfront, beach chairs and umbrellas, bicycles

SURPRISINGLY, BED & BREAKFASTS that sit right on the beach are few and far between. So to discover a place as wonderful as the Elizabeth Pointe Lodge right on Fernandina Beach, one of the most beautiful beaches in the state, is a real treat.

Elizabeth Pointe's twenty-room main lodge looks like an old, turn-of-the-century Cape Cod mansion, with its faded gray shingle sides and its steep, two-pitch gambrel roof. A stand of sea oats on a low bluff are all that separate it from the wide beach and the Atlantic Ocean. The adjacent Miller Cottage has two rooms, and the Harris Lodge has four.

The entire main lodge sits on stilts, so the main floor lobby, breakfast room, and library/sitting room are actually on the second floor. The decor in these rooms continues the Cape Cod motif with nautical accents. A huge stone fireplace, pine floors and paneling, library shelves filled with books, and wicker chairs with overstuffed cushions make these rooms so comfortable, you could spend the whole afternoon there. Panoramic windows offer a spectacular view, particularly at sunset. What looks like an old telescope—but is actually antique Chinese binoculars—sits on a wooden tripod so guests can scan the Atlantic.

It looks like a grand old seaside cottage, but owners David and Susan Caples built Elizabeth Pointe Lodge in 1992. It has all the charm and character of an old place with all the amenities and conveniences of a new one.

Elizabeth Pointe Lodge

I stayed for two nights in the ocean-facing, upstairs suite in the Harris Lodge. It has its own patio and a boardwalk that leads across the low sand dunes to the beach. It is a roomy suite with a king-size bed, comfortably furnished and richly decorated. In the mornings, I walked next door to the main lodge for a delicious breakfast buffet: pastries, muffins, cereals, eggs, French toast, and fresh-squeezed juices.

I spent only two nights at the Elizabeth Pointe Lodge, but I could have stayed for two weeks (or two months) and never wanted for anything.

Amelia Island Williams House
103 South 9th Street
Fernandina Beach, Florida 32034
(904) 277-2328
(800) 414-9257
(904) 321-1325 fax
topinn@aol.com
www.williamshouse.com

8 rooms, $145–225
full breakfast, non-smoking inside, children over 12 welcome, no pets

THE AMELIA ISLAND WILLIAMS House is an antebellum mansion built in 1856. It's namesake, surveyor Marcellus Williams, purchased it three years after it was built. Early folk–Victorian best describes its style. Its signature motif—the elaborate gingerbread on the porch columns designed by Robert Schuyler (the same New York architect who designed the Fairbanks House)— was added in 1880. An ornate, wrought-iron fence surrounds both the Williams House and the Hearthstone annex next door. There are four rooms in the main house and four more in the Hearthstone. All are very elegant, but the Chinese Blue Room seems particularly so, almost as though it was decorated for royalty.

Antiques and valuable works of art are on display throughout both houses. There is even a carpet that once belonged to Napoleon Bonaparte. The elegance continues to the outside, where a gigantic live oak, which might well have been growing before Jean Ribault arrived on the island in 1562, shades the rear garden courtyard.

Hoyt House Bed & Breakfast
804 Atlantic Avenue
Fernandina Beach, Florida 32034
(904) 277-4300
(800) 432-2085
hoythouse@net-magic.net
www.hoythouse.com

10 rooms, $114–159
full breakfast, picnic baskets

BANKER FRED HOYT BUILT this three-story Victorian as his residence in 1905. Walking through the front door is like visiting the zoo. Giraffes of all sizes and colors, sculpted from ceramic, wood, and wicker, guard the lobby. Two rooms that are particularly interesting are the upstairs corner Desert Sunset Room, with its queen-size sleigh bed that sits in a three-sided bay window alcove, and the spacious Sweet Lavender Room, which overlooks St. Peter Church.

The Walnford Inn

102 South 7th Street
Fernandina Beach, Florida 32034
(904) 277-4941
(800) 277-6660
(904) 277-4646 fax
info@walnford.com
www.walnford.com

9 rooms, $95–175
full breakfast, bicycles, non-smoking inside

The Walnford Inn

THE WALNFORD IS ONLY one block away from historic Centre Street. Most of the rooms have Jacuzzi tubs, and some have private balconies. The two rooms that I found most interesting were the Penthouse, which occupies the entire third-floor attic and has a king-size bed and a two-person Jacuzzi, and the downstairs Hemingway Room, which has a king-size, wrought-iron canopy bed with leopard print bedspread and pillowcases, a marble fireplace, and a two-person Jacuzzi also.

Amelia House Bed, Breakfast, and Sail

222 North 5th Street
Fernandina Beach, Florida 32034
(904) 321-1717
(800) 980-3629
www.ameliahouse.com
ameliahouse@net-magic.net

7 rooms, $95–145
full breakfast, day sailing cruises

OWNER BARRY CRONIN RECENTLY added an annex to the main house, which was built in 1865. The annex contains the Captain's Quarters, with two nautical-theme rooms, the Windward Suite and the Leeward Suite. Day sailing cruises are offered aboard the thirty-seven-foot cabin sloop, the Elena.

The Addison House

614 Ash Street
Fernandina Beach, Florida 32034
(904) 277-1604
(800) 943-1604
www.addisonhousebb.com

13 rooms, $115–180
full breakfast, non-smoking (including grounds), one ADA-compliant room

The Addison House

THE ADDISON HOUSE IS actually three buildings that surround a garden courtyard with brick walkways and Mexican fountains. Two of the buildings, the Coulter Cottage and the Garden House, are new structures that are perfect architectural matches with the original 1876 Victorian main house. Each of the rooms is named for a flower. Most have whirlpool baths and canopied or four-poster beds.

The Beech Street Grill
801 Beech Street
Fernandina Beach, Florida 32034
(904) 277-3662

High Springs

IN 1884, THE SAVANNAH, Florida, and Western Railroad extended its tracks from Live Oak south to Gainesville. It passed through a little community known as Santaffey, named after the nearby Santa Fe River. The railroad put up a depot and a post office. Five years later, the townspeople changed the name to High Springs because, at one time, there was a spring on top of a hill in the middle of town.

Nearly a century later, the town was rediscovered as a recreational hub for the surrounding springs and rivers. The Santa Fe River runs right by the edge of town. Poe Springs, Blue Springs, and Ginnie Springs are just a few miles east off of CR 340. O'Lena State Park is just north on Highway 441. Ichetucknee Springs State park is only fifteen miles northeast on Highway 27. High Springs can rightly claim to be at the center of north-central Florida's best springs and rivers. For canoers, kayakers, tubers, scuba divers, and cave divers, it's the ideal destination. It can also be an interesting place to visit for non-aquatic types.

In the mid-1980s, a downtown revitalization began with the restoration of the brick, two-story Old Opera House building (originally built in 1895) on Main Street. Antiques shops, arts and crafts shops, and restaurants began to pop up. Today, downtown High Springs draws visitors daily from around the state. It is a fun place to visit, whether you're a river rat or an antiques hound.

The Rustic Inn Bed & Breakfast
3105 South Main Street (Highway 27/41)
High Springs, Florida 32643-7022
(904) 454-1223
(904) 454-1225 fax
info@rusticinn.net
reservations@rusticinn.net
www.rusticinn.net

6 rooms, $79–89
in-room breakfast basket, pool, hiking path, non-smoking

A TORRENTIAL THUNDERSTORM ROLLED through late on the afternoon of my arrival at the Rustic Inn. I relaxed and read a book while listening to the tranquilizing sound of rain pounding on the metal roof. Sound, or sometimes the lack of it, is one of the Rustic Inn's charms. It sits far enough back from the road that you can't hear what little traffic passes by. In the morning, my only wake-up alarm was the birds singing outside, and I awoke as rested as if I had spent a week meditating at a monastery.

Staying at the Rustic Inn is like visiting a friend's house in the country. The grounds retain the feel of a gentlemen's horse farm, which they once were. A white pasture fence lines the front of the property. There's a horse pasture adjacent to the inn and a forest of planted pine trees, with a hiking path, behind it. In its former life, the inn was a horse stable, although it has been so extensively renovated that you would never recognize it as such.

Larry and Diana Zorovich bought the Rustic Inn in 1996. The Zoroviches are animal lovers, and it shows. Each of the six rooms has a different theme that relates to animals: the Cat Room, the Zebra Room, the Panda Room, the Everglades Room, the Tropical Room, and the Sea Mammals Room. I'm staying in the Cat Room, one of the two end rooms, each with large picture windows. More specifically, the theme is leopards—leopard wallpaper, leopard print shower curtain, jungle scene comforter with, you guessed it, leopards. There is even a stuffed toy leopard kitten that watches over the room from a shelf above the bathroom entry. Beautiful framed prints of leopards and tigers hang on the walls; a "Save the Florida Panther" poster, with a spectacular photo taken by photographer Burton McNeely, is among them. The room is luxurious and a bit exotic, like something I would expect in a five-star lodge in Kenya. It's spacious too—fifteen feet wide and thirty feet long, plus a split-level dressing/vanity/bath area. It has a hand-made, rough-hewn-timber, queen-size bed plus a futon, matching table, and chairs. A copy of *Wild Animals*, a Nature

Library book, sits on the coffee table. Breakfast—quiche, blueberry muffins, bananas, apple and cranberry juices—was left in the room's refrigerator for me to prepare in my room's kitchenette in the morning at my leisure.

Just before I departed, Buddy, the owners' two-year-old chocolate Lab, brought me his tennis ball to play with. They also have two cats and another puppy. With all the animals in residence, it seems fitting that this was once a horse farm.

Grady House

P.O. Box 205
420 NW First Avenue
High Springs, Florida 32655
(904) 454-2206
email@gradyhouse.com
www.gradyhouse.com

5 rooms in main house, $79–99
1 two-story cottage, $175
full breakfast, dinner available at additional cost, non-smoking, children over 8 welcome

---

FROM FIRST AVENUE, THE Grady House, built in 1917, appears as a charming, two-story bungalow. Its twin-gabled front porch has bench swings and wicker chairs. What you don't see are the lush and extensive backyard gardens, with winding pathways and a gazebo with a hammock.

Tony Boothby and Kirk Eppenstein bought the Grady House in 1998. It had previously been a bakery, a boarding house, and an apartment house. Tony and Kirk renovated it and decorated each of the five rooms in a different color. There's the Yellow Room, the Peach Room, the Green Room (which overlooks the gardens), the Navy Room (with a nautical theme and a sitting room with a daybed), and the Red Room. Tony calls this last one the "Nudie Room" since it has over three hundred prints of paintings and lithographs of classic nudes hanging everywhere. All of the rooms are filled with antiques. Some have claw-foot tubs and sitting rooms. It feels very much like someone's grandmother's house (except for the nudes). There's even a portrait of Kirk's grandmother (fully clothed) when she was a 1920s' flapper.

Tony and Kirk recently purchased and renovated the 1896 Easterlin Home next door. They've named it Skeet's Corner Cottage, but it's bigger than the name implies. With two bedrooms upstairs and a family room (with fold-out futon), parlor, kitchen, and private back porch downstairs, there's room for a whole family.

Tony and Kirk serve a home-cooked breakfast and, for an additional fee, a home-cooked dinner. They also serve lemonade all afternoon on the front porch or in the back gazebo. Think of the Grady House as a sanctuary from the much-too-fast-paced outside world. Or just think of it as a visit to Grandma's.

Gainesville

Magnolia Plantation
309 South East Seventh Street
Gainesville, Florida 32601
(352) 375-6653
(800) 201-2379
(352) 338-0303 fax
www.magnoliabnb.com
nfo@magnoliabnb.com

8 accommodations (5 rooms in main house, a duplex —
2 bedrooms each, and a 2-bedroom cottage), $90–160
full breakfast, two-night minimum in cottage and duplexes, fireplaces
in every room, non-smoking, resident watchcats Oliver and Whiner

JOE AND CINDY MONTALTO definitely had their work cut out for them when they took on the task of converting a college "Animal House" into an elegant bed & breakfast. What they found beneath the layers of rubble was a rare architectural jewel.

Victorian French Second Empire architecture was in vogue in the United States from 1860 to about 1890. Ulysses S. Grant commissioned the construction of many public buildings in this style during his presidential administration. It caught on as a fashionable trend in houses too, more so in the Northeast. Grant built his own house in French Second Empire. It even became known as General Grant style—and this is why it did not catch on in the South.

French Second Empire houses are easily recognizable because of their unusual near-vertical mansard roofs, named after French seventeenth-century architect Francois Mansart). Remember The Addams Family house? That's French Second Empire. Restored or well-preserved examples of this architectural style are extremely rare in the South, and a shining example of one that's been restored is the Magnolia Plantation Bed & Breakfast Inn in Gainesville's historic residential section, just east of downtown.

Dudley and Melinza Williams built the house in 1885. Emmett Baird bought it in 1890. The Baird family owned one of the largest wholesale hardware store chains in Florida at the turn of the century and were prominent citizens in Gainesville. They founded the first bank in Gainesville and also built an opera house and a livery stable, which now houses the Sovereign Restaurant. Ownership of the house remained in the Baird family until 1960.

In 1990, Joe and Cindy Montalto bought what had been a student boarding house in need of a lot of work. "The place looked rough," Cindy tells me. "It was filled with trash. Plaster was falling off the walls. It took us until May nineteen ninety-one to open. Joe sanded all the floors. I stripped all the wood-work. We pulled the walls down ourselves. It was a complete gut-and-redo." The results of their labor are astonishing. It ranks among the most impeccable and detailed restorations I've seen.

Today, Joe and Cindy live on the third floor, and the first and second floors are dedicated to the inn. The house has eleven-and-a-half-foot-high ceilings and heart pine floors, and is full of original details, like the corner dust plates on the staircase. There are ten fireplaces, all original. The Montaltos did something very clever in order to retain the original room designs yet give each room its own tub and shower: claw-foot tubs with shower attachments and wraparound curtains occupy a corner or nook inside some of the bedrooms, apart from the bathrooms. In two of the rooms, they actually built bathrooms, or water closets, out of original closets. "You can take a shower, then step out in front of the fireplace to dry off," Cindy points out.

One of my favorite rooms is the Gardenia Room. Cindy calls it the "fluffy room." It has an Eastlake double bed that's as old as the house, and it's one of the rooms that has a water closet. Its bay window overlooks the gardens at the owners' Secret Garden House next door.

Double glass doors lead into the largest room, the Magnolia Room,

Magnolia Plantation

which was the Bairds' master bedroom. A long lounging chair with an elevated headrest sits at the foot of the queen-size bed. Cindy explains that it's called a "fainting couch": "Back then the women wore corsets, and they were so tight that they couldn't breathe, so they had to have some place to lie down and faint!"

On the outside of the house, Joe and Cindy have continued their obsession with authentic detail. The mansard roof with dormer windows has its original fish-scale slate shingles. The flat top of the roof is the original tin. Characteristic of this style of architecture, the house has intricately carved roof cornice brackets, tall, decoratively bracketed windows, and a front entrance double door with a stained-glass window above. A four-story tower with an iron-railed cupola on top rises above the entrance. Cindy and Joe chose different colors to emphasize all the trim details, gingerbread, and bracketing—and there's lots of it. "It is an always-ongoing painting project," Cindy tells me. "We do a side of the house each year. Our painters call it the 'paint-by-numbers house.' They're the only ones that know all the exact colors."

Joe's father is a landscape architect, and they must have really turned him loose, because the grounds at Magnolia Plantation are positively pastoral. Brick pathways wind between huge oak and pine trees, past flowerbeds, and around hedges. There is a pond, a gazebo, and a fountain—all with the dreamlike quality of an idyllic English garden. Joe and his father did most of the actual work themselves, including laying the brick pathways.

In addition to the main house, Joe and Cindy have included a 1950s' duplex next door, which they call the Secret Garden House. They completely remodeled both mirror units, expanding the kitchens/sunrooms out onto enclosed porches, which have Mexican tile floors. Each unit has two bedrooms, a queen-size bed in one room and two twin beds in the other.

Next door, on the opposite side of the main house, is Miss Huey's Cottage, a Cracker house built in the 1870s. Miss Huey was a Shands Hospital nurse who took care of handicapped babies. She lived in the house from 1960 until she passed away in 1994. According to deed records, the house was moved to this spot in 1930 from its original site on Main Street. The original deed indicates that it was a "house of colored rental," which means that it's likely that it was a freed slave's home. Joe and Cindy bought it in 1994 and applied their finely honed restoration skills. It has rocking-chair porches in the front and the rear. The tin-roofed rear porch overlooks more gardens and a fountain where an elephant spews water from its trunk—all shaded by a three-hundred-year-old live oak. Miss Huey's Cottage has two bedrooms (one queen-size and one double bed), a kitchenette, and a fireplaced living room, where Miss Huey's portrait hangs on the wall.

The neighborhood appears to be evolving into Gainesville's bed & breakfast district. Good friends of Joe and Cindy's have purchased the Stick Victorian Lassiter House (circa-1885) next door on the far side of Miss Huey's Cottage. As of this writing, they are restoring it to convert into a bed & breakfast.

A local legend claims that Emmett Baird found pirate treasure buried on the banks of the Suwannee River in the late 1800s. It was supposedly hidden in his house sometime prior to his death in the 1920s. The Montaltos are adamant that there is no hidden booty. If there were, they certainly would have uncovered it during their thorough renovation. Boy, they sure were able to do one heck of a nice restoration, though!

Sweetwater Branch Inn Bed & Breakfast

625 East University Avenue
Gainesville, Florida 32601
(352) 373-6760
(800) 595-7760
(352) 374-3774 fax
www.sweetwaterinn.com
reserve@sweetwaterinn.com

15 accommodations (13 rooms, 1 cottage, and 1 carriage house apartment that sleeps 5), $72–150
full breakfast, non-smoking inside, McKenzie Hall banquet room large enough to accommodate 200 people

Sweetwater Branch Inn
Bed & Breakfast

A COTTAGE, A CARRIAGE house, and two beautifully restored Victorian houses make up the guest accommodations. The Cushman-Colson House (circa 1885) and the McKenzie House (circa 1895) have elements of both Stick and Queen Anne architectural styles, There's also a large reception/banquet hall, a beautiful setting for a wedding. All is surrounded by a full acre of gardens, gazebos, and fountains.

Micanopy

CHARMING SEEMS TO BE the word most frequently used to describe this tiny community. Wide-reaching branches from live oaks form a tunnel over Cholokka Road, Micanopy's main street, as it rolls past aging tin-roofed frame houses. At one time, this was Highway 441, but in the 1960s, the state rebuilt the highway and the Department of Transportation opted to bypass Micanopy. It probably seemed like a death knell then, but it's a godsend now. Micanopy, about ten miles south of Gainesville, is off the beaten path but not too far off.

Downtown Micanopy is an antiquer's paradise. It is only four blocks long, but there are dozens of antiques and curio shops in those four blocks. Most of the buildings date back to the late nineteenth and early twentieth centuries. Huge, ancient oak trees, filled with Spanish moss, shade the entire district.

Micanopy is Florida's oldest inland town. It was established in 1821 and was originally called Wanton's Trading Post. In 1835, the name officially changed to Micanopy in honor of Chief Micanopy, head of the Seminole nation. The town experienced some national fame when the movie Doc Hollywood, starring Michael J. Fox and Julie Warner, was filmed here in 1991.

Herlong Mansion

402 NE Cholokka Boulevard
Micanopy, Florida 32667
(352) 466-3322
(800) 437-5664
info@herlong.com
www.herlong.com

11 rooms, $70–179
full breakfast, fresh-baked muffins and pastries, non-smoking inside, handicap-accessible room, resident ghost

THE HISTORY OF THE Herlong Mansion reads like an Edgar Allen Poe story. It is a place so permeated with intrigue and mystery that you can feel it as you walk up the long brick sidewalk to the front door.

This grand, red-brick Southern plantation house, with Greek Revival architectural characteristics, is appropriately referred to as a mansion. Out front, four massive Corinthian columns support the roof over upstairs and downstairs full-width verandahs. The carefully renovated turn-of-the-century interior has leaded-glass windows; twelve-foot-high ceilings; mahogany, maple, and oak floors; quarter-sawn tiger oak paneling; and ten fireplaces.

Zetty Herlong operated a prosperous lumber business in southern Alabama until one tragic day in 1907, when a fire destroyed both his business and his home. Zetty and his wife, Natalie, moved to Micanopy, into what was originally a simple, two-story, wood-frame house, built some time in the 1840s by Natalie's parents, the Simontons. Natalie had inherited it around the turn of the century. Zetty restarted his lumber business in Micanopy and also became a prominent citrus farmer. In 1909, the Herlongs decided to remodel the old house. They actually constructed the brick version that stands today around the original house.

When Natalie passed away in 1950, her six siblings (four sisters and two brothers) inherited equal shares of the house. They all wanted it for their own, and before long a family skirmish broke out. It seems that none had the resources to buy out the others, except elder sister Inez Herlong Miller, who had inherited a tidy sum from her husband. The bitter family battle would go on for eighteen years. Inez bought out three portions of the house from the estates of two sisters and one brother. The remaining sister refused to sell her one-sixth to Inez at any price but eventually sold it to her brother, who then, in turn, sold his two shares to Inez. Needless to say, the sister was livid. Inez finally owned the house, but the toll on the Herlong Family was incalculable.

The huge mansion had suffered from neglect, and Inez was determined to fix it up. On the very first day of her ownership, while cleaning in one of the rear bedrooms on the second floor (the room that she and her sister Mae had shared during their childhood), Inez collapsed and went into a diabetic coma. Shortly thereafter, she died. Inez would never get to see her long-sought-after house returned to its original splendor.

In 1990, Sonny Howard purchased the Herlong house from Kim and Simone Evans, who had been operating it as a weekend bed & breakfast since 1987. Sonny is an avid traveler. (Be sure to check out his collection of over three hundred canes and walking sticks gathered from his jaunts around the world.) When he became interested in acquiring a bed & breakfast, he looked at castles in Great Britain, mansions in the California wine country, and old homes along the Mississippi River—but none had the character of the Herlong place. Over dinner following the completion of the purchase, Sonny learned from Kim and Simone about some unusual occurrences in the mansion.

Historic restoration specialists from Wisconsin, who were restoring the floors back in 1987, were the first to report odd happenings. They were staying in the house overnight while doing the work. Three nights in a row, they heard footsteps and doors opening and closing on the second floor when no one was up there. On the fourth night, they moved into a motel.

Herlong Mansion

Sonny says, "I was quick to point out to the Evanses that working with drums of paint stripper for three days straight might be more than enough to incline someone to hear ghosts." But the eerie activity didn't end there.

"Nothing scary," Sonny elaborates. "Just odd things, subtle things. Lately we've noticed perfume smells, lilac or gardenia, but only in Mae's Room. We don't use any kind of fragrant cleaners. Sometimes the door to Mae's room locks or unlocks by itself. There have been some odd instances in that room with the window shade, the clock radio, even the Tootsie Rolls that we leave bedside." Sonny himself has heard the door to Mae's room open and close on two separate occasions, when he knew for certain that he was the only person in the house.

Guests and visitors report the most interesting occurrences, usually over breakfast the following morning. Some have vivid and odd dreams. One even saw the image in a mirror of a woman wearing a red shawl.

"Last month a young girl, about three years old, and her mother came in to see the house. The little girl was lively and quite anxious to see inside all of the rooms until she came to Mae's Room. She refused to enter," Sonny relates. Scientists from the Center for Paranormal Studies in Ocala have investigated the ghostly happenings twice. Once they found anomalous electromagnetic readings in the hallway on the second floor. Almost all of the strange occurrences take place in Mae's room or just outside it in the hall. Inez seems to be the likely culprit. If it is Inez, I'm sure she's delighted. The mansion has been beautifully restored, and the interior is filled with antique furnishings. Some have even reported that she looks after guests by tidying up after them, putting their things away in drawers, and locking guest room doors after they turn in. Free help? What bed & breakfast owner wouldn't be happy about that?

Ghostly activity isn't the only unexplained thing about the Herlong Mansion. The building inspector, whom Sonny hired before his purchase, discovered a secret room beneath the house. It's roughly eight feet by eight feet square, and it has no door.

"I think the door might have been where the foundation for the brick house is now," Sonny surmises, "which would mean that it was there prior to the brick house being built. No one knows for sure. There are lots of theories, but no answers. The Evanses thought it might be a hiding place for moonshine, but according to Natalie's surviving brother, V. J., the Herlongs were not drinkers and wouldn't even allow alcohol in the house. V. J. thought it could have been a root cellar that the Simontons had built. But that would be an awful small root cellar. Another theory is that it was a special hiding place, a link in the Underground Railroad (a pre–Civil War secret network of hiding places and people helping fugitive slaves reach freedom). Lastly, some think it might have been a secret meeting room for the Who-Who." Just who were the Who-Who? Apparently they were a closed fraternal order somehow associated with the lumber industry. Reportedly, Zetty Herlong had been active among their ranks.

Sonny's famous gourmet breakfasts are no mystery. He gladly gives out the recipes. Breakfast always includes sides of fresh fruit and homemade muffins. The main courses vary daily. One favorite is Redneck Eggs Benedict, made with scratch biscuits instead of English muffins and American bacon and served with cheese grits, with hollandaise sauce poured over everything. Another is Herlong Decadent Bread, an elaborate version of French toast—it's essentially a baked, French-bread pudding that rises like a soufflé. It's always served with spicy "zinger" sausages.

The house has been extensively restored and renovated. Sonny completely remodeled the third floor, which the Herlongs had originally intended as servants' quarters but had never used. He rebuilt the kitchen and most of the bathrooms, adding claw-foot tubs and showers. He remodeled a downstairs room to be fully handicap accessible. Sonny also converted two outbuildings, the Pump House and the Carriage House, into very cozy cottages. Both have Jacuzzi tubs.

I stayed in Dorothy's Room on the second floor. Like the rest of the house, it is genuinely elegant. It's furnished with antiques and has a fluffy, queen-size bed and an unusual tiled, walk-in shower built from a closet. Double-French doors open onto the spacious upper verandah, furnished with wicker rockers and a big, comfortably cushioned wicker porch swing. Though I didn't get a visit from Inez during the night, I did experience the rare sensation of total peace and tranquillity while I lounged on that porch swing and watched dusk settle into evening.

Shady Oak B & B

203 Cholokka Boulevard
Micanopy, Florida 32667
(352) 466-3476
www.shadyoak.com
goodtimes@shadyoak.com

8 rooms, $75–175
full breakfast, non-smoking inside

FRANK JAMES AND SUSIE Brown built this three-story, old Cracker–style structure in 1989. The bed & breakfast occupies the second and third floors, above the Southern Expressions Gift Shop and the Shady Oak Stained Glass Studio and Ice Cream Parlor. One of the more interesting rooms is Victoria's Room. It has an 1890s' bordello theme, with purple velvet drapes, stained-glass windows, and a Jacuzzi tub.

St. Augustine

AS OLD AND HISTORIC cities go, no continuously occupied city in the United States is as old, and few are as historic, as St. Augustine, Florida.

Spain considered Florida its own after 1513, when Ponce de León landed on the eastern shore and claimed it (the theory of the month says it was somewhere near Melbourne). In 1562, French explorer Jean Ribault landed at the mouth of the St. Johns River, near present-day Jacksonville, and began claiming that land for France. This angered the Spanish, even though they had paid little or no attention to Florida for the previous half century. So, in 1565, King Philip II of Spain sent Pedro Menendez de Avile and an army of seven hundred men to kick the French out of Florida, a successful mission. Menendez arrived on the northeast coast of Florida on the Feast Day of St. Augustine and celebrated with a mass, then named the place in honor of St. Augustine. It grew into a village and eventually the city of St. Augustine.

St. Augustine's early Spanish settlers didn't have it so great. Florida was a very harsh environment to settle in—lots of swampland, mosquitoes, snakes, alligators, and Indians, who, for the most part, weren't very happy that the Europeans had invaded their territory. As if all that were not enough, they also had to contend with pirates and an occasional invasion by the British. I'm sure some of the original Spanish settlers wondered, Why did we fight so hard for this?

In 1702, the British invaded and burned the entire St. Augustine village to the ground. That's why the Oldest House, the Gonzalez-Alvarez House on St. Francis Street, dates back to 1702. Historians estimate that it was constructed shortly after the destructive fires.

Much of the city's development took place following Henry Flagler's arrival in the mid-1880s. Don't miss seeing the magnificent Flagler College, which was originally Henry Flagler's Ponce de Leon Hotel. For more detailed information about that period, see A Tale of Two Henrys.

If you can look beyond some of its touristy aspects, St. Augustine's historic district is a fascinating place to visit today. Narrow brick avenues and alleyways separate coquina concrete and wooden buildings, many dating back to the 1700s. Balconies hang out over the streets. Horse-drawn carriages clip-clop along the roads. The district has the quaint look and feel of an old English village; some of the older structures were actually built during British occupation. A few streets, like St. George, have been cordoned off for pedestrians. There are lots of cafés, galleries, antiques shops, and, of course, lots of bed & breakfasts, so many that sometimes you'll find several in a row. There are five at the north end of Cordova Street alone, all next door or across the street from each other.

Centennial House Bed & Breakfast, St. Augustine

The south end of the historic district is the oldest section of the city and is where the Oldest House is. It's far less commercial and less crowded than other areas, and a lot of people miss it, but a stroll at this end is well worth the effort. Also, don't miss the Castillo de San Marcos National Monument. Earliest construction on this fortress dates back to 1672.

Centennial House Bed & Breakfast
26 Cordova Street
St. Augustine, Florida 32084
(904) 810-2218
(800) 611-2880
(904)810-1930 fax
cenhouse@aug.com
www.centennialhouse.com

7 rooms, $100–205
full breakfast, two-night stay minimum on weekends, children over 16 welcome, handicap-accessible room, non-smoking

STEVEN BRUYN KNOWS A little bit about evaluating a market segment and determining the customer's wants and needs. He should—he was a senior marketing and product development manager with Chrysler Corporation (now Daimler-Chrysler), where he worked on future car projects. So it is no surprise that when Steven, his wife, Rosemary, and son, John, decided to get into the bed & breakfast business, their very first step, before hammering a single nail into the house, was to gather data from consumer opinion surveys and focus groups to ensure that they would create something that would match inn-goers' desires.

In 1997, the Bruyns came across a hundred-year-old, two-story frame house at the corner of Cordova and Saragossa Streets, a great location—in the middle of St. Augustine's historic district. But the house was dilapidated. It would require more than a restoration; it would have to be completely reconstructed.

The house was close to collapse. "The floor upstairs bounced so much we called it the trampoline," Steven explains. "In some places, the floor joists were within an inch of falling through. The house had been subject to a hundred years of rot, termites, and neglect. We spent fourteen months rebuilding the entire building. The roof joists were the only major component that we could reuse. Everything else, including the framing, had to be built new." The Bruyns were able to recycle some of the disassembled materials. Four original chimneys, too fragile to leave standing, had to be taken down. So they reused the antique bricks to build a petite tropical courtyard beside the house.

Steven and his family are gracious hosts, and I end up spending the better part of an afternoon with them. Steven tells me, "My guess is that the family that owned (the house) must have lost all their money in the Crash of Twenty-nine because in the early nineteen-thirties it became a rooming house. And it deteriorated steadily from that point on."

The finished product, completed in 1999, is what the Bruyns describe as their "brand new hundred-year-old building." It's historically and architecturally accurate, but with modern electrical and plumbing, bathrooms and updated kitchen fixtures, whirlpool baths, gas fireplaces, high-tech air conditioning, handicap accessibility, fire alarms, and sprinklers—hence their tag line, "19th-century city living, 21st-century luxury."

Although ninety percent new, this is still a historic building. Much had to be done to maintain the house's historical integrity. The Bruyns were fanatical about attention to historic details. For example, Steven had all sixty-four original, single-glaze (independent pane) windows in the house removed and shipped to a company that dips them. Some didn't survive the process, so he replaced those with new, custom-built, single-glaze windows that are exact replicas of the originals. The renovation work is impeccable, inside and out.

Centennial House
Bed & Breakfast

The final result of all their labor is a warm and inviting inn, with both modern amenities and turn-of-the-century charm. It sits just two blocks north of Flagler College, once Henry Flagler's beautiful Ponce de Leon Hotel. Cordova Street is part of the carriage route, and the inn's enclosed sunroom on the first floor gives guests a perfect panoramic view of the passing horse carriages.

The Centennial House has five rooms upstairs and one downstairs, as well as a suite upstairs in the Carriage House behind the main house. All benefit from Rosemary's creative decorating. One very clever idea that was incorporated into some of the bathrooms was to create sink vanities out of antique dressers and tables. The complete rebuild allowed the luxury of designing a second floor that makes full use of spacious rooms and bathrooms. The Bruyns also installed special sound insulating material in the walls.

The Main Room, downstairs in the main house, is fully ADA-compliant and includes a roll-in shower, wider doors, and easy-to-open door handles. Steven's attention to detail shines again: he made the room compliant while he maintained a Victorian look and atmosphere.

All the rooms are palatial, but I particularly like the Gentleman's Quarters, with its gas fireplace, Jacuzzi tub, and walk-in shower. Another favorite room—and the most requested—is the Safari Room. It has carved sculptures of elephants and giraffes, a two-person Jacuzzi tub in the corner, a king-size, wrought-iron bed, and a gas fireplace.

The Carriage House was a circa-1930s garage and apartment. The Bruyns knocked out the attic floor to give the building fourteen-foot-high cathedral ceilings. Although I missed seeing the interior because it was occupied, Steven describes the Carriage House suite as L-shaped, with a sitting area, a fireplace, and French doors leading onto its own deck.

The Bruyns like to serve a grand, gourmet breakfast. Guests feast on entrees like frittatas, pan perdu (baked French toast stuffed with peaches), Welsh rarebit, and a variety of soufflés. They never have the same dish twice in a week.

Steven retired from Daimler-Chrysler in 1999. He tells me, "My opinion is that we're all going to live to be a hundred years old, so now when you hit your fifties, you have to ask yourself what are you going to do for the second half? I knew mine was going to be really different from the first half. St. Augustine is a great city to invest in. I've always liked restoration, and I'd like to do some more here." No doubt there's more to come from the Bruyn family.

St. Francis Inn

279 St. George Street
St. Augustine, Florida 32084
(904) 824-6068
(800) 824-6062
(904) 810-5525 fax
innceasd@aug.com
www.stfrancisinn.com

14 accommodations (9 rooms and 2 suites in the main inn, 1 cottage, and 2 suites in the Wilson House), $79–219 full breakfast, pool, bicycles, non-smoking, complimentary admission to St. Augustine's Oldest House

THERE IS "OLD" IN St. Augustine, and then there is "very old." The St. Francis Inn falls into the latter category. It was built in 1791 and is one of only a few original true Spanish Colonial–architecture buildings left in Florida. While it has not functioned continuously as an inn, this is likely the oldest building that is currently an inn in St. Augustine.

Just eight years after Spain reacquired Florida from Great Britain, Spanish infantry sergeant Gaspar Garcia built his home in St. Augustine on land granted to him by the king of Spain. It was not unusual for Spain to grant property to soldiers as a reward for meritorious duty. During those tumultuous times, houses were built to withstand attack. Garcia built his from thick coquina limestone (not unlike the walls of nearby Fort Castillo de San Marcos), flush with the corner formed by what are now St. Francis and St. George Streets. The only problem was that those two streets did not cross at a precise right angle. To make the house fit, Garcia built it in a slightly trapezoidal shape. As a result, there are no perfectly square or rectangular rooms in the inn. The slightly out-of-square footprint of the house is evident in the angle of the floorboards.

St. Francis Inn

Current owners Joe and Margaret Finnegan have compiled a thorough chronology of prior owners of and additions to the house. Many of the owners have been military figures, like British Marine colonel Thomas Dummett, who purchased it in 1838. The colonel's daughter, Anna, was the first to convert the home into an inn. Anna's brother-in-law, Confederate major William Hardee, purchased it in 1855, then sold it to John Wilson in 1888. It was Wilson who added the third floor and mansard roof to the main inn. He also built several surrounding buildings, including the Wilson House across the street, which houses two suites for the St. Francis Inn. From 1894 on, the main house was variously rented as a residence or as apartments and was also operated as a hotel. It was owner Ralph Moody who gave it the name St. Francis Inn in 1948.

Manager Mary Sparks took me on a tour of some of the notable rooms. Elizabeth's is a two-room suite with a large sitting room and a kitchenette cleverly built into a former closet. It overlooks St. Francis Park across the street. Anna's Room is smaller but has access to the balcony that sits above the inn's shaded courtyard and a St. Francis of Assisi statue and fountain. All the first- and second-floor rooms have fireplaces. The inn was hosting a wedding party the day I visited, and they were taking pictures in the Balcony Room. This is the inn's premier room, with floor-to-ceiling windows, a two-person Jacuzzi, and its own private balcony.

The Finnegans purchased the St. Francis in 1985. In 1996, they renovated the inn's interior. Recently, they added something unusual for a small historic inn or bed & breakfast—a schedule of Sunday evening folk music performances.

In his book *Ghosts of St. Augustine* (Pineapple Press, 1997), author Dave Lapham reports that the St. Francis Inn has a ghost. As legend tells it, Major Hardee's son and Lilly, a black slave, were madly in love, something considered taboo in those days. The young Hardee, distraught over their dilemma, committed suicide—but he is not the ghost. It is Lilly who has been seen walking the halls of the St. Francis Inn.

Secret Garden Inn
56¹/² Charlotte Street
St. Augustine, Florida 32084
(904) 829-3678
www.secretgardeninn.com

3 suites, $85–165
in-room Continental breakfast, kitchen and private entrance
in each suite, non-smoking inside

ARTIST NANCY NOLOBOFF USED to have her own business making handcrafted clowns. For a while she sold real estate. Then, in 1991, she opened the Secret Garden Inn. Secret Garden comes from the Frances Hodgson Burnett children's book by the same name, in which ten-year-old Mary Lennox discovers a secret garden. Estabon and Eva Alvarez bought the inn from Nancy in 2000.

As the name implies, it is a secluded, almost hidden spot, despite its location in the precise center of St. Augustine's historic district. Its inconspicuous entrance, tucked away behind a swinging gate off Charlotte Street, leads down a narrow, hedge-lined walkway into the Secret Garden's courtyard. Palm trees, banana trees, and a small jungle of plants, vines, and flowers—ginger, wisteria, hibiscus—surround the three-room inn.

The circa-1920s, bungalow-style structure was built as a guest cottage for the house that sits in front of it on Charlotte Street (which now houses Vin-Tiques, a wonderful antiques shop). Four-and-a-half-foot-tall Marie

Kitchen Ward was the original owner of both. Marie, a popular singer in her day, was billed as the Songbird of the South. In her later years, she lived downstairs in what is now the Secret Garden Inn's Hibiscus Suite, until she passed away at age ninety-seven.

Each of the three suites—Hibiscus, Wisteria, and Moon-flower—has its own outside entrance, kitchen, and private patio or upstairs deck. All are decorated with original artwork. Hibiscus, the largest suite and the only one downstairs, is bright with flower prints and has a brick patio that opens onto the garden. I am staying in the Moonflower. Although it is the smallest, I think it is the most charming. Its one room has windows on three sides, a vaulted ceiling with triangular windows in the peaks, a kitchen and bathroom at one end, and a queen-size bed at the other.

Secret Garden Inn

Sunlight (or moonlight), filtered by the surrounding branches, streams through the windows. Visually, it seems as though I am in a tree house. Me Tarzan, you Jane.

There is no dining room. The idea here is privacy. At the Secret Garden Inn, they take the term "bed & breakfast" quite literally and deliver breakfast to each room. My Continental breakfast includes croissants, blueberry and apple-spice muffins, cheese, guava jam, cantaloupe, strawberries, and a carafe of orange juice.

For the most part, I have not included bed & breakfasts so small that they have only three rooms. I've made an exception for the Secret Garden Inn because its exquisite intimacy comes in great part from its diminutiveness. Lee, who manages the inn for Estabon and Eva, tells me that the owners have plans to add three more rooms, for a total of six, but that they will be extremely careful to do it in a way that preserves the place's charm.

Casa de Suenos Bed & Breakfast

20 Cordova Street
St. Augustine, Florida 32084-3619
(904) 824-0887
(800) 824-0804
(904) 825-0074 fax
(800) 735-7534 fax
info@casadesuenos.com
www.casadesuenos.com

6 rooms, $85–190
full breakfast, live weekend music, bicycles, resident golden retriever,
Spice, and cat, Charm, portion of proceeds donated to Florida School
for the Deaf and Blind

BY THE TURN OF the twentieth century, the Colee family had been in the
carriage business in St. Augustine for fifty years. Originally a stagecoach
company, the family business evolved into Colee's St. Augustine Transfer
Company, whose horse stables were across the street from William Colee's
house, now the Casa de Suenos.

Casa de Suenos Bed & Breakfast

William's brother, James, a surveyor for Henry Flagler, built the house in 1904. It was originally a one-and-a-half-story clapboard cottage. In the 1920s, cigar manufacturer Patalina Carcaba purchased it and completely remodeled it into a Mediterranean–Spanish Eclectic style with varied-height, flat roofs; parapet walls; and tall, arched windows—an architectural style that it retains today. It was an office building when Ray and Sandy Tool bought it in 1994. It took the Tools a year to renovate, adding bathrooms (three with whirlpool tubs) and decorating lavishly to suit the Spanish style and the 1920s era. Sandy, who has a background in food and hospitality management, had a clean slate to which to apply her talents. The name Casa de Suenos (House of Dreams) reflects Sandy's lifelong dream to own her own inn. Ray's background is chemistry, and he now formulates his favorite concoctions in the kitchen. Guitarist Holly Mulkey plays on weekend and holiday evenings. Holly also painted the picture of Casa de Suenos that hangs in the foyer. Cordova Street is part of St. Augustine's Carriage Route, and horse-drawn carriages rolling past the Casa de Suenos make for a scenic image that will transport you back to 1900.

Casa Monica Hotel

95 Cordova Street
St. Augustine, Florida 32084
(904) 827-1888
(800) 648-1888
(904) 827-0426 fax
casamonica@grandthemehotels.com
www.casamonica.com

137 rooms including 50 suites, $129–599
restaurant, lounge, pool, exercise room, sidewalk café/deli/
coffee and dessert bar

ON JANUARY 1, 1888, Boston entrepreneur and architect Franklin Smith opened the Casa Monica Hotel on property he had purchased from Henry Flagler. He constructed it at the same time and in a similar architectural style—Spanish Renaissance with Moorish Revival elements—as Flagler's St. Augustine hotels, the Ponce de Leon (now Flagler College) and the Alcazar (now the Lightner Museum). Actually, Flagler borrowed the style from Smith.

Less than four months after Smith's hotel opened, Flagler bought it from Smith and renamed it the Cordova. In 1902, Flagler built a bridge between the Cordova and his Alcazar Hotel next door, making them one hotel. St. Johns County bought the original Cordova structure in 1962 and, over the next two years, remodeled it into the St. Johns County Courthouse.

Casa Monica Hotel

In 1997, Richard Kessler, central Florida hotelier and former CEO of Days Inns of America, bought the courthouse and spent two years on a complete restoration. Kessler, who now owns Grand Theme Hotels, brought it back to its original Flagler-era splendor and reopened it in 1999 as the Casa Monica Hotel.

Casa Monica resembles a palace as much as a hotel. The exquisite restoration included rebuilding the original hotel's carriage entrance. The elegant lobby features a bronze fountain, antique chandeliers, and historic maps and original artwork on the walls. The rooms have Spanish wrought-iron beds and mahogany furnishings. Each of the Casa Monica's five towers is a multistory luxury suite.

Casa de La Paz Bayfront Bed & Breakfast

22 Avenida Menendez
St. Augustine, Florida 32084
(904) 829-2915
(800) 929-2915
delapaz@aug.com
www.casadelapaz.com

6 rooms, $120–225
full breakfast, resident cats, Garfield and Frosty

CASA DE LA PAZ translates in Spanish to House of Peace, and you will have plenty of that, along with quiet and relaxation, at this immaculate bed & breakfast. The three-story house is a rare but classic example of Mediterranean Revival–Italian Renaissance architecture, with characteristic arched windows and doorways and hipped, red-tile roof with decorative eaves brackets. It was built in 1915 as a private residence for banker J. D. Puller (whose ghost, reportedly, still resides here). It served as apartments from the mid-1950s until the mid-1980s, when Harry and Brenda Stafford bought it and turned it into a bed & breakfast.

Kramer and Sandy Upchurch bought it in 1990 and did even more extensive restoration. Current owners Bob and Donna Marriott, after owning and operating a bed & breakfast in North Carolina for several years, purchased the Casa de la Paz in 1996.

The house has magnificent views overlooking Matanzas Bay and the Bridge of Lions across Avenida Menendez. Of the six rooms, the favorite has to be the Captain's Quarters, a loft with sitting room that occupies the entire third floor. Guests can see all the way to the Atlantic Ocean from the sitting room's dormer windows. Among the myriad antique furnishings is the Marriotts' collection of forty-seven antique music boxes.

Casa de La Paz Bayfront Bed & Breakfast

Breakfast is an event at Casa de la Paz, with entrees like stuffed French toast, blintz soufflés, and all varieties of pancakes. Baking is one of the Marriotts' specialties, and fresh-baked muffins and cakes are available throughout the day. Don't plan to stick to your diet when you stay here.

Kenwood Inn

38 Marine Street
St. Augustine, Florida 32084
(904) 824-2116
(800) 824-8151
(904) 824-1689 fax
www.oldcity.com/kenwood

14 rooms and suites, $85–185
non-smoking, no small children, two-night minimum stay on
weekends, three-room suite on third floor

Kenwood Inn

THE KENWOOD IS A superb example of mid-nineteenth-century Victorian architecture, with a wide, two-story verandah that wraps around three sides. Claw-foot bathtubs and four-poster beds (some with canopies) continue the Victorian theme in each of the rooms. The house was built in 1865, presumably as a private residence, and converted into a boarding house/inn in 1886. Owners Mark, Kerrianne, and Caitlin Constant tell me that makes it the oldest continuous-operation inn in St. Augustine. Its location, in the less-hectic southern end of the historic district, is only a block west of the waterfront and a block north of St. Augustine's Oldest House.

Casablanca Inn Bed & Breakfast

24 Avenida Menendez
St. Augustine, Florida 32084
(904) 829-0928
(800) 826-2626
904-826-1892 fax
casablanca@aug.com
www.casablancainn.com

14 rooms including eight suites, $89–225
full breakfast, non-smoking inside, children over 12 welcome

FOLLOWING THE PROHIBITION ACT of 1919, St. Augustine became a busy booze-smuggling port. During the 1920s, the Casablanca was the circa-1914 Matanzas Hotel, and U. S. Treasury Agents were regular patrons. An elderly woman, who remains anonymous, owned the Matanzas at that time and apparently had an arrangement with smugglers (for a fee, of course) who were bringing their contraband into Matanzas Bay by night. If no agents had checked into the hotel that evening, she would climb up onto the rooftop widow's walk and wave a lantern as an "all clear" signal. After fourteen years of Prohibi-tion, the innkeeper reportedly died a very wealthy woman. Legend claims that her ghost still waves a lantern, late at night, from the roof of what is now the Casablanca Inn.

The second-floor Anniversary and Celebration Suites have private porches with double hammocks that overlook Matanzas Bay across Avenida Menendez.

Casablanca Inn Bed & Breakfast

Cedar House Inn

Cedar House Inn

79 Cedar Street
St. Augustine, Florida 32084
(904) 829-0079
(800) 233-2746
(904) 825-0916 fax
russ@aug.com
www.cedarhouseinn.com

6 rooms including one suite, $89–174
full breakfast, bicycles; owner Russ Thomas, a notary public,
can perform marriages at the inn

RUSS AND NINA THOMAS left their Ft. Lauderdale jobs (his with BellSouth, hers in the medical profession) to get into the bed & breakfast business in St. Augustine. In 1990, they bought a circa-1890s three-story Victorian on Cedar Street. They rented it as a duplex for a while before jumping in with both feet. In 1993, they opened the Cedar House Inn with only two rooms to rent and have continued to improve it and add on to it. Their continuing restoration has included adding all new electrical, air conditioning, a new telephone system, wraparound porch, a gazebo, and six bathrooms.

Saragossa Inn Bed & Breakfast

Original owner Carl Decker, a carpenter and builder who came to St. Augustine to take part in the Henry Flagler development boom, built the house in 1893. Decker built this house as his own and four others in the surrounding neighborhood on speculation. It has been a private residence, a rental property, and, for a while in the 1970s, a fraternity house for Flagler College.

Saragossa Inn Bed & Breakfast
34 Saragossa Street
St. Augustine, Florida 32084
(904) 808-7384
(904) 808-1203 fax
lindan@aug.com
www.oldcity.com/saragossa

6 rooms, $79–120
full breakfast

THIS CRAFTSMAN-STYLE BUNGALOW was built in 1920, and restored and converted into a bed & breakfast in 1990. Four of the six rooms have two beds, which makes the Saragossa well suited for families. The Fireplace Room is a two-room, two-bed suite made from the original living room.

Victorian House Bed & Breakfast
11 Cadiz Street
St. Augustine, Florida 32084
(904) 824-5214
(877) 703-0432
(904) 824-7990 fax
info@victorianhouse-inn.com
www.victorianhouse-inn.com

8 rooms, $75–125
full breakfast, non-smoking, bicycles, children welcome
in Carriage House

ALBERTO ROGERO'S ANCESTORS WERE from Minorca, one of the Baleares Islands off the east coast of Spain. They had settled in St. Augustine a century before Alberto built this house in 1897. Current owners Ken and Marcia Cerotzke left their corporate management and sales jobs to purchase it in 1999. The previous owner, Daisy Mordan, had done a major restoration in 1983 that included adding bathrooms to each room.

The Inn on Charlotte Street Bed & Breakfast
52 Charlotte Street
St. Augustine, Florida 32084
(904) 829-3819
(904) 810-2134 fax
www.innoncharlotte.com

5 rooms, $75–145
full breakfast

THE ENGLISH COUNTRY HOME ambiance of the Inn on Charlotte Street is a fitting reflection of innkeeper Vanessa Wyatt Noel's British heritage. Vanessa moved to the United States in the 1960s. She operated inns in New Hampshire and Maine before coming to St. Augustine.

The two-story brick house was built between 1912 and 1914 for attorney—and later St. Augustine's mayor—Levi Nelson. The large front porch with wicker rocking chairs and porch swing invites guests to sit and read or sip tea. Vanessa says her Matanzas Room, on the second floor, is her most romantic, with its own fireplace, two-person Jacuzzi tub, and a porch view overlooking Matanzas Bay and the Bridge of Lions.

The Inn on Charlotte Street
Bed & Breakfast

Bayfront Westcott House

146 Avenida Menendez
St. Augustine, Florida 32084
(904) 824-4301
(800) 513-9814
info@westcotthouse.com
www.westcotthouse.com

9 rooms, $115–225
full breakfast, afternoon wine, non-smoking inside, bicycles

THE CIRCA-1880 WESTCOTT House's location, at the south end of Avenida Menendez where it curves west into St. Francis Street, affords the inn's guests terrific views of Matanzas Bay.

Dr. John Westcott came to St. Augustine in the 1850s and soon became involved in its development, particularly where transport was concerned. One of his projects, the St. Johns Railroad, ran tracks from the San Sebastian River, which runs right through St. Augustine, to the town of Tocoi, to the west on the St. Johns River. He was also instrumental in creating the Intracoastal Waterway, which runs through Matanzas Bay right in front of his house.

Bayfront Westcott
House

Westcott House was restored and converted into a bed & breakfast in 1983. Robert and Janice Graubard purchased it in 1999. All of the rooms are furnished with turn-of-the-century antiques, and some have their own fireplaces. Most have views of the bay, but the best view is from one of the big wicker chairs on the front porch.

Old Powder House Inn
38 Cordova Street
St. Augustine, Florida 32084
(904) 824-4149
(800) 447-4149
(904) 825-0143 fax
kalieta@aug.com
www.oldpowderhouse.com

8 rooms, $79–165
full breakfast, afternoon
hors d' oeuvres and wine,
10-person Jacuzzi, chil-
dren over 8 welcome,
non-smoking inside

THE HOUSE THAT IS NOW
the Old Powder House Inn was
originally built in 1899. It sits
on property where, a century
before that, soldiers ware-
housed gunpowder during the
second Spanish occupation of
St. Augustine, hence the name.

Old Powder House Inn

Agustin Inn
29 Cuna Street
St. Augustine, Florida 32084
(904) 823-9559
(800) 248-7846
agustin@aug.com
www.agustininn.com

7 rooms, $89–135
full breakfast

Alexander Homestead
14 Seville Street
St. Augustine, Florida 32084
(904) 826-4147
(888) 292-4147
(904) 823-9503 fax
bonnie@aug.com
www.oldcity.com/alexander

4 rooms, $125–175
full breakfast

Southern Wind Inn

Aunt Peg's Bed & Breakfast

89 Cedar Street
St. Augustine, Florida 32084
904) 829-0076
auntpegs@aug.com
www.staugustineinns.com/auntpeg.htm

6 rooms including two suites in Carriage House, $95–135
full breakfast, non-smoking

Southern Wind Inn

20 Cordova Street
St. Augustine, Florida 32084
(904) 825-3623
(800) 781-3338
swind@aug.com
www.southernwindinn.com

10 rooms, $79–185
full breakfast, non-smoking

Carriage Way Bed &
Breakfast

Carriage Way Bed & Breakfast

70 Cuna Street
St. Augustine, Florida 32084
(904) 829-2467
(800) 908-9832
(904) 826-1461 fax
bjohnson@aug.com
www.carriageway.com

9 rooms, $69–130
full breakfast, children welcome in some rooms
(call to inquire),
non-smoking inside

Whale's Tale
Bed & Breakfast

Whale's Tale Bed & Breakfast
54 Charlotte Street
St. Augustine, Florida 32084
(904) 829-5901
(888) 989-4253
whale@aug.com
www.oldcity.com/whale

7 rooms, $89–149
full breakfast, non-smoking inside

St. Augustine Beach

Coquina Gables Oceanfront Bed & Breakfast
1 F Street
St. Augustine Beach, Florida 32084
(904) 461-8727
(904) 461-4346 fax
gables@aug.com
info@coquinagables.com
www.coquinagables.com

6 suites, $119–189
full breakfast, pool, 8-person Jacuzzi, beachfront, bicycles,
shuffleboard court, non-smoking, children over 15
welcome in Garden House

Coquina Gables Oceanfront

THE COQUINA GABLES OFFERS something that is inexplicably rare in Florida—a beachfront bed & breakfast. Aubrey and Tracy Arnn bought the 1926 home and the Garden House behind it and converted them into a bed & breakfast in 1999. Turn off A1A down a little side road, F Street, and it dead-ends at the Coquina Gables and the beach. The two-story main house, pink with white trim, is thought to have originally belonged to one of Henry Flagler's attorneys. Dark, rich wood paneling and floors give the three main house suites the feel of an African safari lodge. All three have king-size beds and ocean views. A central upstairs great room has massive Honduran mahogany beams spanning its ceiling. It opens onto an enclosed sunporch with a panoramic view of the beach and the Atlantic Ocean.

Light colors decorate the three contemporary Garden House suites, and all have queen-size beds. The Arnns have named their rooms after famous authors: Ernest Hemingway, F. Scott Fitzgerald, Zane Grey, Sinclair Lewis, Agatha Christie, and William Faulkner.

In front of the Garden House and next to the main house are a large swimming pool and deck, a screened-in cabana with an eight-person hot tub/spa, and something no old beach house in Florida is complete without—a shuffleboard court.

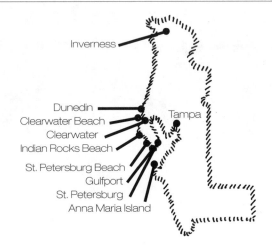

Inverness

Dunedin
Clearwater Beach
Clearwater
Indian Rocks Beach

St. Petersburg Beach
Gulfport
St. Petersburg
Anna Maria Island

Tampa

CENTRAL WEST

BRUCE HUNT

Don CeSar Beach Resort and Spa, St. Petersburg Beach

Inverness

THIS WEST-CENTRAL FLORIDA, hill-country town was originally named Tompkinsville, but the name was changed to Inverness in 1889. Local legend claims that an emigrant Scotsman (whose name no one can recall) became homesick while standing on the banks of Lake Tsala Apopka, adjacent to Tompkinsville. It reminded him of the lake country near his home, Inverness, Scotland. At least one report claims that the Scotsman was one of the many phosphate-boom speculators who swarmed to central Florida in the late 1880s and early 1890s, and that he offered to donate $2,000 toward the construction of a new courthouse if town officials would change the name of the town.

Inverness' one-block-long Main Street, with the historic Citrus County Courthouse marking its east end and the twenty-foot-tall Bank of Inverness clock at its west end, is a vibrant district with restaurants, galleries, and shops.

The Crown Hotel
109 North Seminole Avenue
Inverness, Florida 34450
(352) 344-5555

33 rooms, $70–75
full breakfast, two restaurants, pub, pool

THE CROWN HOTEL, A white, three-story wooden structure with burgundy canvas awnings over its windows, reminds me of a Scottish country club. But this now-dignified inn had humble beginnings.

Inverness was once known as Tompkinsville. The rough-and-ready Tompkins brothers, post–Civil War Confederate soldiers, settled here in 1868. The Crown began life as a general store when Alf, one of the Tompkins brothers, gave his brother-in-law, Francis Dampier, property on which to build a store. Dampier built the store on one side of Bay Street and his home on the other. Sometime around 1900, Dampier moved his store to Main Street, and in 1907, he turned it into a boarding house called the Orange Hotel. Ten years after that, he sold it to a New York hotel syndicate, which, in 1926, moved it again, this time around the corner to Seminole Avenue, its present location.

In conjunction with the move, the New York group performed what must have been an amazing feat of construction in its day. They built an entirely new bottom floor, then hoisted the original two-story building onto the new first floor, making a three-story hotel: the Colonial.

Crown Hotel

The Colonial was a popular place for a number of decades, but by the 1970s it had fallen into serious disrepair. It had recently been condemned when, in 1979, Reg Brealy came to Inverness, representing a British company called Epicure Holdings. They had sent him to look at another piece of property, but he convinced them that the Colonial was the real jewel-in-the-rough. They bought it for a reported $100,000 and spent the next year and a half—and an additional $2 million—completely restoring it in the style of a fine English residence. They also built a new restaurant and kitchen and added a swimming pool.

The Crown is everything a British inn should be: regal, stately, and elegant, with an interior decorated in forest greens, burgundies, and, of course, royal blues. A crystal chandelier hangs from the ceiling in the lobby atrium. A wide, curving, one-piece floating staircase sweeps around the chandelier up to the second floor landing. Lithographs depicting British countryside hunting scenes hang from hallway walls. Beneath the stairs, a glass case displays an exact replica of the Crown jewels. Epicure Holdings purchased the set from one of the few British companies licensed to reproduce them.

Office manager Terrie Adkisson has worked at the Crown Hotel since its grand reopening in 1981. She recalls the restoration: "It was a total reconstruction. Except for a few items like antique light fixtures, everything that went in was new. This beautiful wood staircase was custom-built in North Carolina and shipped in one piece. It arrived the same day as the chandelier."

The hotel even had its own authentic 1909 double-decker bus, an Inverness landmark that sat parked in front of the Crown for many years. "Epicure bought the double-decker bus at an auction in London and had it shipped to Portsmouth, Virginia," Terrie tells me. "One of the gentlemen who was going to help with its restoration flew up to Portsmouth, then drove it all the way down to Inverness—in the middle of winter! The bus is right-hand drive. The driver's compartment is completely open—there's not even a windshield. And it ran at a top speed of about thirty-five miles per hour! In nineteen ninety-seven, we donated it to the city. They are re-restoring it, and it will be on permanent display on a new brick bus pad that will be built downtown."

Epicure sold the Crown Hotel in 1985, and it sold again in 1990 to the current owners, Nigel and Jill Sumner. The Sumners, originally from Manchester, England, operated a seaside hotel in Wales before moving to Inverness and acquiring the Crown. "The Sumners are hands-on, working owners," Terrie tells me. "At any given moment you might find her working down in the laundry room, and he might be washing dishes in the kitchen." The personal care they have taken with the inn shows. The Crown exudes English fastidiousness.

The elegant Churchill's Restaurant, on the first floor of the Crown Hotel, is perhaps better known than the hotel itself. Regular diners come from as far away as Ocala and even Tampa just for Sunday dinner, according to Terrie. Friend and fine restaurant connoisseur Dr. Clyde Asbury once told me that you can always judge a restaurant by its soup. If the soup is exceptional, so will be the rest of the meal. This was indeed the case at Churchill's. I started my dinner with the chicken and rice soup, which sounds rather ordinary but is not. It was creamy and thick, almost chowderlike, well spiced and filled with carrots, celery, potatoes, and large tender chunks of chicken breast. Then, for an appetizer, I had rumaki, which is chicken liver wrapped in bacon, baked, and, in this case, floating in a savory mild brown sauce.

My entree was unmistakably British and very tasty: braised veal kidneys and steak tenderloin, sautéed in onions and bacon, with a rich bourbon gravy. Fresh green beans and a baked potato rounded out the plate.

For lunch the following day at the Crown's Fox and Hound Pub, I had split-pea soup and curried chicken over wild rice with chutney, sliced almonds, raisins, and shredded coconut on the side. Don't let anyone tell you that the Brits prefer bland food—this meal was full of flavor. The menu features other traditional British fare, such as homemade English sausages with mash, cottage pie, and steak and kidney pie. The Fox and Hound's atmosphere and decor are, naturally, British/Scottish pub.

The forty-six-mile-long Withlacoochee State Trail, which runs roughly from Trilby in the south to Dunnellon in the north, comes to its approximate halfway point in Inverness. It passes through just a couple blocks north of the Crown. "The trail brings us a lot of business," Terrie explains. "Bicycle tours regularly make the Crown their lunch stop or overnight stop."

Shops, galleries, and more restaurants are only a block away on Inverness' nicely restored downtown Main Street. There are other restored historic structures nearby. Two that are noteworthy are the old 1911 Citrus High School, now the Administration Office for the Citrus Memorial Hospital, and the old Citrus County Courthouse, which, as of this writing, is in the process of being restored by the Citrus County Historical Society.

The Lake House Bed and Breakfast

8604 East Gospel Island Road
Inverness, Florida 34450
(352) 344-3586

5 rooms, $80–120

THE LAKE HOUSE IS a restored fishing lodge on the shores of Big Lake Henderson, about twelve miles east of Inverness.

Dunedin

J. O. Douglas House Bed & Breakfast

209 Scotland Street
Dunedin, Florida 34698
(727) 735-9006
(877) 642-2623
(727) 736-0626 fax
sclaus@gte.net
www.jodouglashouse.com

4 rooms, $85–110
Continental breakfast, pool, bicycles, non-smoking, wheelchair accessible, two rooms have shared bath, currently open full-time in winter and weekends the rest of the year

J. O. Douglas House
Bed & Breakfast

JOHN OGILVIE DOUGLAS AND James Somerville, immigrants from Scotland, came to Jonesboro, the original name of Dunedin, in the early 1870s. They opened Douglas and Somerville General Store, which competed with another store and trading post opened a couple years earlier by George Jones, for whom Jonesboro was named. Douglas and Somerville petitioned for and were granted an official U. S. post office in their store in 1878. In the petition, they submitted the name Dunedin. Two theories offer explanations for their choice. First, Dun-Edin is Gaelic for "town of St. Edena, or Edinburgh, the capital of Scotland. Second, Douglas and Somerville abbreviated and combined their respective hometowns, Dundee and Edinburgh, and arrived at Dun-Edin.

Although they were business rivals at first, John Douglas and George Jones ultimately became good friends and together were instrumental in the development of Dunedin. An 1889 plat shows that Jones owned much of the property on both sides of what is now Main Street, and Douglas owned large plots south of that.

In 1878, Douglas built his Queen Anne Victorian home at the corner of Edgewater Drive and Scotland Street, just down the street from the abandoned cotton gin warehouse that housed his general store. It was the first house in the area built from machine-cut lumber planks, which were shipped from Cedar Key. Today it is the beautifully restored and landscaped J. O. Douglas House Bed & Breakfast. It is listed on the National Register of Historic Places and is considered the oldest standing house in Dunedin. Sherril Claus has owned it since 1997 and has furnished it with some unusual antiques: a century-old English chifforobe, a Victorian fainting couch, a Chinese whale oil lamp, and an 1860 mahogany Willcox and White Reed Parlor Organ. Rocking chairs, a porch swing, and a hammock make the screened porch a great place to kick back. The gray house with white trim, surrounded by a white picket fence, sits in Dunedin's historic residential neighborhood. From the front yard, you can look across Edgewater Drive to the city park and beyond that to St. Joseph Sound and the Gulf of Mexico. One block north is Dunedin's pedestrian-friendly, renovated historic Main Street, with Victorian street lamps, brick walkways, shops, galleries, and restaurants (one of my favorites is the tiny but superb Black Pearl Restaurant).

The Black Pearl Restaurant
315 Main Street
Dunedin, Florida 34698
(727) 734-3463

Clearwater Beach

Clearwater Beach Hotel
500 Mandalay Avenue
Clearwater Beach, Florida 33767
(800) 292-2295
(727) 441-2425
cbhotel@msn.com
www.clearwaterbeachhotel.com

159 rooms, $79–249
restaurant, lounge, pool

IN CONTRAST TO ITS spring break–motivated surroundings, the five-story Clearwater Beach Hotel stands in defiant elegance at the north end of Clearwater Beach. The hotel's sparkling white, nautical-style architecture and white, wood, and brass interior befits a luxury ocean liner as much as it does a hotel.

The Clearwater Beach Hotel, most likely the oldest hotel on the beach, originated as a two-story vacation beach cottage built by the Roux family (who owned a lumber company in Bartow) shortly after the turn of the century. Within a couple of years, Mrs. Roux converted it into a boarding house. Over the past century it has been added on to and rebuilt numerous times. At one point, probably during the 1920s, it became a school with sixty dormitory rooms. Although the Roux family no longer occupied it, they still held the mortgage. In the mid-1930s, in the depth of the Great Depression, New Yorker Goodman Kelleher bought the devalued property from them and added a thirty-eight-room north wing. In 1944, Kelleher sold it to another New Yorker, Maurice Pauchey, who added twelve more units on the beach. Ed Hunter, whose family had been coming to the hotel since the 1920s, along with managing partner Boss Hotels, bought the hotel in 1955. The Clearwater Beach Hotel still remains in the Hunter family.

The Hunter family has added and renovated quite a bit over the past half century. In its current version, the Clearwater Beach Hotel reflects the classic sophistication that it had in the 1950s, when black-tie events took place in the ballroom. But it manages to artfully balance this with the casualness of a beach place. The hotel sits on a wonderful beach, one of the widest expanses of white sand on the Gulf of Mexico—often hundreds of yards wide down to the water at low tide. In the main hotel are rooms with private balconies, many overlooking the swimming pool and the gulf. Two

Clearwater Beach Hotel

additional, two-story wings house efficiencies, also with balconies and views. Just south of the property is a third building of oceanfront suites with kitchenettes. The hotel's gourmet restaurant serves entrees like broiled Norwegian Salmon with grilled prosciutto and fried shallots in cabernet sauce, and peppered ostrich with pan-seared ostrich sausage, shiitake mushrooms, merlot sauce, caramelized pear, and cranberry dressing.

Clearwater

Belleview Biltmore Resort & Spa
25 Belleview Boulevard
Clearwater, Florida 34617
(800) 237-8947
(727) 442-6171
(727) 441-4173 fax
rooms@belleviewbiltmore.com
www.belleviewbiltmore.com

292 rooms, $89–1500
pool, three restaurants, pub, golf, tennis, spa

Belleview Biltmore Resort & Spa

AS I PASS THROUGH the guard gate at the Belleview Biltmore, I am reminded of some of the grand hotels in the northeast, particularly the Mount Washington Hotel at Bretton Woods in the White Mountains of New Hampshire (it was completed in 1902, five years after the Belleview). Two things grab my attention at the front of the Belleview: the magnificent, two-hundred-year-old oak tree that stands next to the entrance, and the attractive (but architecturally incongruent) glass octagonal lobby, which Hideo Kurosawa added in 1990 during the hotel's $10-million renovation.

The Belleview Biltmore is a colossal, rambling structure. The largest occupied wooden building in the world, it's white with green, steep-gabled roofs. (Henry Flagler's Royal Poinciana Hotel in Palm Beach was larger, but it was dismantled in 1935.) It has 292 guest rooms and suites on five floors. Two miles of hallways crisscross its interior, and six square miles of carpet cover the floors. Painters used over a million gallons of paint to cover its exterior prior to 1975, when aluminum siding was installed. It also has a basement designed as an elaborate network of corridors, some with narrow-gauge tracks for handcarts so hotel employees can transport supplies, maintenance equipment, and luggage out of sight of guests (long before Disney employed the same concept at Disneyworld).

The Belleview Biltmore's grounds are as neatly manicured as the Belleair Country Club's golf course next door. Original developer Henry B. Plant had trees and shrubs brought in from as far away as South America and Africa. Some flourish on the south lawn.

Henry Plant, railroad and steamship magnate and founder of Plant Investment Company, understood that to entice travelers to use his Florida railroad lines, he would need to offer them plush accommodations along the way. His trains ran from Charleston, South Carolina, through Savannah, Georgia, and Jacksonville, Florida, and terminated in Tampa. His shipping lines picked up in Tampa and ran through Key West down to Havana, Cuba.

Plant built eight lavish resorts; the Belleview is the only one that still functions as a hotel. It was to be more than just a hotel. Plant wanted the Belleview to be a palace where he could entertain dignitaries and wealthy railroad and shipping clients. He commissioned the design of an entire community, Belleair, to surround and support it. Construction began in 1895. Plant purchased the Orange Belt Railroad, which he connected with his existing line, and ran tracks to the site of his newest hotel. When the Belleview opened on January 15, 1897, it had 145 rooms, telephone and telegraph service, and electric lights. An orchestra played concerts each day. Plant's guests—some of whom arrived by their own private Pullman rail cars—played golf, rode horses, sailed, and shot skeet. It was as lavish as he had envisioned it would be, but he would enjoy it for only two years. Henry Plant died in June 1899.

A personality who was perhaps even more interesting than Henry Plant was his son, Morton. Morton took over the operation of Plant Investment Company and the Belleview following his father's death. Two of his first improvements to the hotel were to reroof it with green shingles and to repaint the exterior white. Next he built a series of private cottages on the hotel property. In 1909 and 1910, he added the east wing (which doubled the room capacity), a new kitchen, and a dining room to the hotel.

Morton also expanded the golf course to a full eighteen holes. Golf was becoming an important attraction at the Belleview, and in 1915, Morton hired famous golf course architect Donald Ross to redesign the existing course and add a second eighteen-hole course. Most Florida golf courses at the time had sand greens, but Morton wasn't satisfied with that. He experimented with various types of soils, fertilizers, and grasses until he found a combination that would function in Florida's climate. The Belleview's golf courses were the first in this region to feature grass greens.

In 1912, Morton's young son, Henry II, was seriously injured when he was thrown from an automobile during an accident. There were no hospital facilities nearby, so Morton had a railroad car converted into a small hospital with equipment brought in from Chicago. A full-time doctor and a staff of nurses spent three months overseeing young Henry's recuperation. As a result of this experience, Morton donated $100,000 toward the creation of a hospital in Belleair in 1914. The twenty-one-room Morton Plant Hospital was completed in 1916.

Despite all of Morton Plant's accomplishments, the most frequent footnote to his life's history concerns his unusual second marriage. In 1914, one year after his wife of twenty-five years, Nellie Capron Plant, died, Morton became enamored of Maisie Manwaring. The only problem was that Maisie was married and had a son. Morton's solution was to offer Maisie's husband $8 million to divorce her. Her husband accepted, and Maisie and Morton married in 1914. Shortly thereafter, Morton adopted her son, Philip.

In 1916, Maisie saw a fifty-four-inch strand of nine-millimeter cultured Oriental pearls at Cartier's in New York. She insisted on having the necklace, but Morton wouldn't buy it for her, claiming that $1.2 million was too much to spend on a strand of pearls. Undeterred, she returned to the famous jewelry store and negotiated with Pierre Cartier to trade her opulent 5th Avenue townhouse, which Morton had given her as a wedding present, for the pearls. Cartier's still owns the townhouse.

John McEntee Bowman with the Biltmore Hotel chain purchased the Belleview in 1919, following Morton Plant's death the previous year. Bowman spent over $1 million to expand the hotel again, adding a south wing and enlarging the Tiffany Room dining hall. In the 1920s, with "Biltmore" now added to its name, the Belleview remained true to Plant's original vision of extravagance by attracting the wealthiest and most famous of patrons: Vanderbilts, DuPonts, and Studebakers, not to mention Walter Hagen, Gene Sarazin, Bobby Jones, and Babe Ruth. But the high times would not last.

With the 1929 stock market crash and Bowman's death in 1931, the Biltmore Hotel chain went bankrupt. Creditors took over operation of the Belleview until 1939, when Kirkeby Hotels operator Arnold Kirkeby purchased it.

World War II brought a dramatic change to the Belleview. During 1942 and 1943, the U.S. Army Air Corps converted the lavish hotel into temporary barracks to supplement permanent facilities at MacDill and Drew Fields in Tampa. All the lavish furnishings were put into storage. The windows were painted black to prevent the building from being spotted at night by enemy submarines in the Gulf of Mexico. The hotel housed three thousand troops.

One benefit of this conversion was that the Army insisted on having a fire sprinkler system installed. Ironically, workers completed the $100,000 system the day the troops moved out.

In 1944, with troops vacated, Kirkeby sold the empty hotel at auction to St. Petersburg real estate developer Ed Wright for a paltry $275,000. In 1946, Wright sold the still-empty and deteriorating hotel to a group of Detroit investors: Bernard and Mary Powell, Nora Peabody, and Roger Stevens, who was part-owner of the Empire State Building. Theirs was the daunting task of reviving the Belleview to its past grandeur. It reopened in 1947, but renovations continued for ten years after that. In 1975, they covered the exterior with aluminum siding to drastically lower their painting expenses without altering the hotel's appearance. In 1986, they added the spa and fitness center and the indoor pool.

Hideo Kurosawa of Mido Corporation in Japan bought the Belleview in 1990 for a purported $27.5 million. The lobby needed to be revised to conform to new handicap-accessibility requirements, and Kurosawa took the opportunity to build a completely new lobby and front entrance. While in itself the new structure is not unattractive, many people have criticized it for having virtually no architectural tie to the main hotel. Kurosawa also added a golf clubhouse and four clay tennis courts and replaced the aging outdoor pool with a two-hundred-thousand-gallon, barbell-shaped pool complete with elevated hot tub and its own waterfall.

In 1997, the Jetha family, owners of the Bass Company in Vancouver, Canada, purchased the hotel from Kurosawa and revived the old name, Belleview Biltmore.

My room was an antique-furnished, two-room suite on the third floor. It had a giant balcony that overlooked the gorgeous swimming pool, Clearwater Bay beyond the hotel grounds, and the private Belleair Country Club golf course to the south. I wanted to take some interior pictures of the seemingly endless hallways and decided to wait until well after midnight, when things would be quietest. I took several shots on various floors and didn't see another soul. Then I moved down to the first-floor main hall off the lobby. It's kind of a spooky experience to be the only person awake in this enormous hotel. While I set up my tripod, a bellboy transferring luggage for a late arrival wheeled around the corner and startled me. "Keep your eyes open. I think I saw Jack Nicholson down the hall a little while ago," he said with a sly grin. He was joking about the movie version of Steven King's *The Shining*, but at 2:00 A.M. in this otherwise empty hallway in the Belleview, I almost believed him.

The following morning, I walked down that same hallway, now filled with hotel guests heading to the pool, or to the spa, or to the tennis courts.

The hallway contains the hotel's shops: The Four Seasons Florist, News on the Corner, 'Round the World Gifts, Royal Sports Sportswear, Tissy's Boutique, Biltmore Photography—there's even a Stamas Yacht dealer, Yacht World. Halfway down the hall, I found the Belleview Biltmore Historical Museum. Much of the hotel's history, as well as the history of the community of Belleair, is chronicled here in old photographs and documents. One item on display that I found very interesting was a circa-1930s Simplex movie projector, which was used to show movies in the Starlight room here half a century ago. The hotel conducts daily historic tours from the museum at 11:00 A.M.

Also off of this hallway are the Belleview's two ballrooms—the grandly appointed Tiffany Room, which seats eight hundred people as a dining hall and has ninety-six leaded-glass ceiling panes, and the equally grand but smaller Starlight Room. The far end of the hall leads to the Terrace Café and Patio Restaurant and the St. Andrews Pub downstairs.

The list of luminaries, dignitaries, and celebrities who have recently vacationed at the Belleview is long and varied: Margaret Thatcher, George Bush, the Duke of Windsor, the Beach Boys, Caroline Kennedy, and George Foreman, to name a few.

Indian Rocks Beach

One Fifth Avenue Indian Rocks Beach
1 5th Avenue
Indian Rocks Beach, Florida 33785-2520
(800) 876-5302 ext. 02
(813) 254-6964 fax
chriscorral@irbbeachfront.com
www.irbbeachfront.com

2 accommodations:
3-bedroom main house, $170 per night (5-night minimum stay), $3,700 per month
beachfront, king-size bed in master suite, twin beds in other t
wo bedrooms, large kitchen, screened front porch overlooking Gulf of Mexico, large breezy Florida room, herb garden

Carriage house studio efficiency, $80 per night (3-night minimum stay), $1,650 per month
king-size bed, kitchen, second-floor porch with gulf view

ALTHOUGH IT IS TECHNICALLY neither an inn nor a bed & breakfast, I've included this Indian Rocks beach house because it holds a very special place in my heart and in my memory. It is a piece of my personal heritage.

Some of my earliest childhood memories are of summers spent at Grandmommy and Granddaddy's beach house, a two-story, brick-patterned stucco-fascia bungalow built in 1915. It was one of the first to go up on Indian Rocks Beach. Granddaddy bought it in 1945. My brother, sister, cousins— we all spent the majority of our summer days here. I can close my eyes and still smell the aroma of salt air–weathered wood. I can still feel the give in the hardwood pine floors. I can still hear Grandmommy playing "Rock of Ages" on her old upright piano in the Florida room in the afternoon. (I could even hear her all the way out at the end of Dr. Myer's pier next door while I fished for sheepshead around the pilings.) I can still see the magnificent electrical storms out on the gulf—jagged tentacles and spider webs flashing from one end of the horizon to the other—that I watched in the evenings from the screened front porch. And I can still taste graham cracker cookies slathered with peanut butter and washed down with Coca-Cola, a staple in Grandmommy's beach diet.

In the 1970s, a high-rise developer began buying property on Indian Rocks Beach, intending to knock down some of the old houses to make way for multi-story condominiums. Granddaddy had passed away several years before,

One Fifth Avenue
Indian Rocks Beach

and I guess the developer thought Grandmommy would be glad to sell the house. She said no. The developer became desperate. He upped his offering price and said he would also give her a choice of the condo units! Her response? "No, thank you."

My cousin Chris Corral owns the house now. He spent two solid years restoring it. It was the kind of careful renovation that only someone with a deep emotional attachment to a place could possibly do.

My grandmother passed away in 1989. She was 91, or 92, or 93, or 94—no one knows for certain, because she would never divulge precisely what year she was born. But she still lives, and is a vibrant driving force, in our hearts. And she most certainly still lives in the beach house.

Gulfport

Sea Breeze Manor Bed & Breakfast Inn
5701 Shore Boulevard
Gulfport, Florida 33707
(888) 343-4445
(727) 343-4445
(727) 343-4445 fax
www.seabreezemanor.com

7 rooms, $95–150
full breakfast, non-smoking, no children

LOCAL GULFPORT RESIDENTS USED to call it the "Storm House," because, with its twelve-inch-thick walls, it was the safest place to seek sanctuary during a hurricane. Built in 1923, it remained a private residence until Patty and Lawrence Burke purchased it in 1996 and opened the Sea Breeze Manor. The Burkes were construction contractors before getting into the bed & breakfast business. By the looks of the Sea Breeze, they must have been very good at their job. The restoration and remodeling are exceptional. Every detail, inside and out, is perfect.

The Sea Breeze Manor fits perfectly in quaint, colorful Gulfport, a tranquil arts community on the shores of Boca Ciega Bay. Tiny Gulfport is self-contained but is also encapsulated within the big city of St. Petersburg. Galleries, antiques and arts-and-crafts shops, and restaurants (including one of my favorites, the Backfin Blue Café) line Beach Boulevard, Gulfport's main street, for a half dozen blocks.

Sea Breeze Manor
Bed & Breakfast Inn

Painted sea green with white trim and a bright red roof, the house combines Tudor architecture with a dash of the Caribbean—thanks to tropical landscaping, green-and-white striped umbrellas, and Bahamian shutters. There are four suites in the main house, plus an attached cottage on the west side of the house and a detached cottage on the northwest side (once a schoolhouse the original owners built for their disabled child). A lush garden courtyard separates this cottage from the house.

Each room is named for an exotic tropical location, which is appropriate. The Sea Breeze Manor reminds me of a luxury villa on St. Barthélemy or in the British Virgin Islands. I am staying in the Jamaica Suite on the second floor. Exotic-locale decor graces the interior—a faux zebra skin lampshade, a huge ceramic elephant paperweight, lush live potted plants in the bedroom and bathroom. Colorful, tropical-scene paintings hang from the walls. French doors open onto the room's private wraparound balcony with Adirondack chairs—a perfect place to spend the morning watching pelicans soar over the bay. The bathroom is enormous—ten feet by twelve feet—and has a stand-up shower, a separate tub with its own window (overlooking the bay, of course), and a pedestal sink, all with new modern fixtures.

Ah, yes—the bed! The king-size bed has a European-style, four-inch-thick, quilted baffle-box feather bed on top of its mattress. I sank into it up to my ears, and it gave me the most wonderful, most restful night's sleep that I've had in a decade. Listening to the soft lapping of the waves on Boca Ciega Bay probably helped.

Not only are the Burkes renovation and decoration perfectionists, they're apparently also cleanliness nuts. I cannot find a speck of dust in this place—not even along the top of the chair rail!

Breakfast, which I opted to have out on the Sea Breeze's verandah (overlooking the bay, of course), begins with coffee, fresh-squeezed orange juice, and a bowl filled with pink grapefruit, strawberries, nectarines, and cantaloupe. The second course was fluffy pancakes cooked with peaches and coconut in the batter, then dusted with powdered sugar, and maple-cured bacon on the side. The finishing course was a cinnamon-walnut pastry.

The Sea Breeze Manor is an immaculately restored, impeccably clean, luxurious, exotic, and romantic escape. Comments that I read in my room's guest book tell it all: "Like being away on a tropical island on the other side of the world;" ". . . a little bit of paradise."

Backfin Blue Café
2913 Beach Boulevard
Gulfport, Florida 33707
(727) 343-2583

St. Petersburg Beach

Don CeSar Beach Resort and Spa
3400 Gulf Boulevard
St. Petersburg Beach, Florida 33706
(727) 360-1881
(800) 637-7200
(800) 282-1116
(727) 367-6952 fax
www.doncesar.com

345 accommodations (including 50 suites and 2 penthouse suites in main hotel and 70 suites in Beach House Suites); a sister property one half mile north, $169–1,574

beach, three restaurants, three bars, spa and health facility, two pools (one with an underwater sound system), shops, kayaks, catamarans, waverunners, aqua bikes, and the world's best ice cream parlor (Be sure to visit Betty Hammond: she makes the very best sundaes!)

THE PINK PALACE, THE Pink Elephant, the Wedding Cake. I knew it as the Pink Monster while I was growing up in Tampa in the 1960s. It was a crumbling and blatantly unmaintained government-owned building that housed, among other things, a regional Veterans Administration office. When the government abandoned it in 1969, there wasn't much pink left. Afterward, it just deteriorated into a hulking, boarded-up ghost castle. Rumors abounded that it was haunted. It had been an Army hospital in the early 1940s, and the entire eighth floor had been converted into operating rooms. Stories circulated (at least among my elementary school friends) that late at night you could still hear screams from the top floors—screams of the ghosts of combat soldiers having limbs amputated without sufficient anesthesia.

It sat unattended for several years, subject to vandals, vagrants, and the elements. Eventually Pinellas County officials decided that they would put a park there, if the federal government would just blow the old building up. That was when a group of local residents formed a "Save the Don" committee. Spurred on by newspaper articles written by June Hurley, they made it their mission to find a buyer who would restore the building. They found that buyer in St. Petersburg Beach Holiday Inn owner William Bowman Jr., who bought the old Don in 1972 for a reported $400,000. The restoration was a monumental undertaking. The work was tedious: thirteen thousand panes of original glass had to be removed, scraped, and reinstalled. Bowman went to great lengths to be as historically accurate as possible but also needed to update the building with modern conveniences such as central air conditioning and new plumbing and electrical systems. The refreshed Don CeSar Hotel opened on November 24, 1973, although it took almost two more years to complete all of the restorations and to have the hotel placed on the National Register of Historic Places.

The Don CeSar Hotel has become the symbol of St. Petersburg Beach. The ten-story, ultra-pink, stucco Mediterranean Revival structure is clearly visible from the Sunshine Skyway Bridge ten miles south. Six towers with belfry arches rise from its red, barrel-tile roofs. Red-and-white striped awnings shade balconies and penthouse terraces. A wide driveway that bridges Gulf Boulevard leads to the front entrance of the second-floor lobby. Inside, marble floors, arched entryways, soaring ceilings, chandeliers, and grand pianos lend an air of 1920s' opulence. You would feel right at home in a tuxedo, although most people walking through the lobby are wearing shorts and T-shirts over bathing suits. The beach side of the Don CeSar is a paradise, with pools, tiki bars, palm trees, and bougainvillea vines. It all spills out onto the glistening white beach lined with red cabana beach chairs.

Don CeSar Beach Resort and Spa

Thomas J. Rowe was a Norfolk, Virginia, real estate broker who was in poor health and living from month to month when he moved to St. Petersburg in 1919, just in time for the land boom. Within six years, both his health and his financial situation had improved immensely. In 1925, he bought eighty acres, some of it beachfront, at the north end of Passe-A-Grille (south St. Pete Beach) from developer Perry Snell. Rowe's original plan called for a residential neighborhood of Spanish-style homes, but he also wanted a centerpiece, a grand hotel. To generate cash in order to build his hotel, he began subdividing the property and selling off lots.

Construction began on the hotel in 1925. Rowe hired contractor Carleton Beard and Indianapolis architect Henry DuPont. Halfway into its completion, Rowe fired DuPont because the hotel looked too plain. Rowe and Beard had traveled to Boca Raton and Miami and admired the architecture of Addison Mizner and George Merrick. That's what they wanted. They decided that they could do without plans—they would design the rest of the hotel as they built it. The Don CeSar opened with much fanfare on January 16, 1928. It was a huge success in its first twenty months, until October 29, 1929—the stock market crash. Occupancy dropped to a fraction of what it had been, and Rowe could not meet his mortgage obligations. The hotel went into receivership, but Thomas Rowe was still allowed to manage it. He worked night and day and, despite poor economic times, managed to build up business once again. At one point, he signed up the New York Yankees for a three-year contract of spring training seasons. For a while, Lou Gehrig, Babe

Ruth, and other ballplayers were regular faces at the Don CeSar. Other famous (sometimes infamous) guests included F. Scott Fitzgerald, Clarence Darrow, Franklin D. Roosevelt, even Al Capone.

By the end of the 1930s, Thomas Rowe had paid off his debts and once again owned the hotel. Then, in May 1940, he died. He had asked his lawyer to draw up a new will that would leave the hotel to his employees, but he passed away before signing it. Mary Rowe, Thomas' estranged wife (they had been separated for decades), inherited the Don CeSar. She had never even set foot in it before. Mary appointed her attorney, Frank Harris, as president of the corporation that ran the hotel. One year later, World War II broke out, and business plummeted again. Harris was negotiating a deal to lease the hotel to the United States Navy as officers' residences when, without warning, the government condemned the hotel and allowed the Army to buy it for its paltry, tax-assessed value of $450,000. The Army turned it into a hospital, and in the early-mid 1940s, it was converted into an Air Force psychiatric/convalescent hospital. The Veterans Administration moved in in 1945.

Today, everyone knows the Don CeSar Hotel as simply the "Don." Don Caesar De Bazan (yes, the spelling is different), by the way, is a fictional hero in the Vincent Wallace opera *Maritana*. In an odd parallel to the hotel's own history, in *Maritana*, Don is ordered by Spain's King Charles II to be executed by firing squad, but the guns misfire and he lives! Apparently Thomas Rowe was a fan of the opera, or at least a fan of a young Spanish opera singer named Lucinda, whom he had met in his younger years. Hotel staff sometimes report seeing a man who resembles Thomas Rowe from old photos walking the hotel grounds late at night with a beautiful, dark-haired Latin woman. Maybe the Don is haunted.

St. Petersburg

ST. PETE NO LONGER CARRIES the reputation as an "old folks' retirement town." Oh, it's still a great place to retire, but the city, particularly its downtown, has undergone a major revitalization. St. Pete now has one of the most vibrant and pedestrian-friendly downtowns of any major city in Florida. Fine restaurants, outdoor cafés, galleries, upscale shops, parks, and museums—including the Florida International Museum, the Salvador Dali Museum, and the Museum of Fine Arts—have turned St. Petersburg into a fascinating destination.

Renaissance Vinoy Resort

501 Fifth Avenue Northeast
St. Petersburg, Florida 33701
(727) 894-1000
(800) 468-3571
(727) 894-1970 sales office fax
(727) 822-2785 guest fax
www.renaissancehotels.com/TPASR/

360 rooms, $165–349
four restaurants, health club and spa, golf course, tennis courts, croquet courts, marina, sailing charters and school, two pools, two ballrooms, non-smoking rooms available, handicap-accessible rooms available

TRANSPLANTED PENNSYLVANIA OIL BARON Aymer Vinoy Laughner thought the property across the street from his St. Petersburg home had a lovely view of Tampa Bay and would make the perfect location for a luxury hotel. He bought the property in 1923 and in 1925 built his Spanish-Mediterranean Vinoy Park Hotel in just ten months. It had 375 rooms and cost $3.5 million to build. It opened on New Year's Eve and was a lavish palace of a hotel in an age when the well-to-do and the well-known liked to travel to lavish palaces in Florida. In its day, the Vinoy hosted DuPonts, Guggenheims, and Pillsburys. Herbert Hoover, Jimmy Stewart, Babe Ruth, and F. Scott Fitzgerald were regular guests. When World War II broke out, Laughner leased the hotel to the Army Air Corps, then reopened it in 1946. Shortly after, he sold it to Charles Alberding, who upheld the Vinoy tradition of grandeur well into the 1950s.

Sadly, in the 1960s, a lack of regular maintenance as well as a lack of air conditioning took its toll on the Vinoy. By the end of the 1960s, it had lost much of its luster. By the early 1970s, it had declined into a low-rent (reportedly $7 a night) boarding house. It closed down in 1974.

Laughner's once-grand hotel sat boarded up and deteriorating for sixteen years. In the late 1980s, the Vinoy was scheduled for demolition, then saved from the bulldozers at the last minute when it was purchased in 1990. Two years and $93 million later, it was reopened as the Stouffer Vinoy. The renovation was a marvel. Restorers saved much of the original detail work and recrafted what they couldn't save. The hand-stenciled, pecky-cypress ceiling beams in the lobby were restored, as were the Pompeii-theme frescoes on the exterior and dining hall walls. Workers also made some

Renaissance Vinoy
Resort

needed changes and additions. Rooms in even the most extravagant hotels built in the 1920s were very small by today's standards. In the 1990 reconstruction, every three rooms were remodeled into two, and an additional 102-room tower was built to bring the total number of rooms up to 360.

Renaissance Hotels and Resorts, a division of Marriott Hotels, bought Stouffer Hotels in 1993 and currently own and operate the Vinoy. Today, it is every bit as elegant as Aymer Vinoy Laughner intended it to be. No doubt, he would be pleased.

Heritage Inn

234 Third Avenue North
St. Petersburg, Florida 33701
(727) 822-4814
(800) 283-7829
(727) 823-6144 fax
floundee@aol.com
www.holidayinnstpete.com

71 rooms, $89–149
pool, restaurant, banquet room

Heritage Inn

THE HERITAGE INN WAS the Martha Washington Hotel when it opened in 1926. It is now affiliated with Holiday Inns. Cypress Hotel Management, out of Orlando, recently purchased it. It has undergone several remodels and upgrades, all of which give the Heritage Inn a flavor of its original era.

Julien's Restaurant, located next door and owned by the hotel, was previously the much-touted Heritage Grille, which enjoyed a decade-long reputation for fine food and for fine art hanging on the walls. I hope the new owners will uphold that tradition. One interesting historical tidbit—the ornate wooden bar in Julien's came from the house of Confederate President Jefferson Davis.

Mansion House Bed & Breakfast
105-115 Fifth Avenue NE
St. Petersburg, Florida 33701
(727) 821-9391
(800) 274-7520
(727) 821-6906 fax
mansion1@ix.netcom.com
www.mansionbandb.com

13 rooms, $95–165
full breakfast, pool, murder mystery weekends June–October, boat cruises, non-smoking

TWIN, MIRROR-IMAGE BUNGALOWS, built in 1904 and 1912, and an adjacent carriage house comprise Rob and Rosie Ray's Mansion House Bed & Breakfast in the Old Northeast residential district just north of downtown St. Petersburg. Both two-story bungalows have white stucco on the first floor exterior, pastel peach shingle siding on the second, and aqua green awnings and trim. One of the bungalows was the home of St. Petersburg's first mayor, David Moffett. The other belonged to a Dr. Kemp. In the mid-1920s, another doctor, R. K. O'Brien, bought both, using one as his office and the other as his residence.

Alan and Suzanne Lucas moved from their home in Wales, Great Britain, to St. Petersburg in 1991. They bought and renovated the 1904 house and converted it into a bed & breakfast. After Rob and Rosie purchased it from the Lucases, they expanded the inn in 1998 to include the second bungalow.

Bring your appetite. The Rays are fond of hearty breakfasts, with items such as blueberry pancakes, French toast, omelets, and fresh-baked bread. Something extra—Rob arranges cruises for guests on his twenty-three-foot *Aussie Spirit.*

Mansion House
Bed & Breakfast

The Claiborne House
340 Rowland Court NE
St. Petersburg, Florida 33701
(727) 822-8855
(800) 281-4090
www.claibornehouse.com

9 accommodations (5 rooms and 4 suites), $95–115
full breakfast, stocked refrigerators in rooms, handicap-accessible
room available, non-smoking

WHAT WAS THE BAY Gables Bed & Breakfast is now the Claiborne House. The Faust family, which also owns the Claiborne House in Charleston, South Carolina, recently purchased it. The St. Petersburg Claiborne House, built in 1910, is a three-story structure with wraparound verandahs on each level. It's a short, half-block walk to Straub Park and the waterfront on Tampa Bay.

The Claiborne House

Bayboro House
Bed & Breakfast

Bayboro House Bed & Breakfast

1719 Beach Drive SE
St. Petersburg, Florida 33701
(727) 823-4955
(877) 823-4955
(727) 823-4955 fax
bayboro@gte.net
www.bayborohousebandb.com

7 rooms (4 in main house and 3 in carriage house), $125–165
Continental breakfast, pool, non-smoking inside,
children over 12 welcome

BAYBORO HOUSE WAS ST. Petersburg's first bed & breakfast. Gordon and Antonia Powers had owned the sprawling mansion since the early 1970s and began operating it as a bed & breakfast in 1982. Dave and Sandy Kelly purchased it in 2000.

Built in 1907, Bayboro House was the home of Charles A. Harvey, a Georgia real estate developer who owned most of the property in this early St. Petersburg neighborhood known as Old Southeast Bayboro. The neighborhood's brick streets and gracious turn-of-the-century homes sit across from Lassing Park and overlook Tampa Bay. Harvey's original plan included building a harbor here on Tampa Bay, but he died in 1914 before he could initiate that project.

The nineteen-room house blends Queen Anne Victorian style with Shingle Victorian elements such as shingle-clad gables and bay windows with polygonal roofs. Two life-size stone lions sitting on pedestals guard its wide front steps. The side entrance is flanked by stalking lions. Dave was glad to give me a tour of the house and rooms. All the rooms in the main house have bay windows or large picture windows and are generously furnished with antiques. My favorites are the second-floor Harvey Room—with a king-size, mahogany, four-poster canopy bed and a bay window that actually looks out over a bay, Tampa Bay—and the Williams Room, next to it, with a picture window and the same view.

Bayboro Inn and Hunt Room
357 3rd Street South
St. Petersburg, Florida 33701
(727) 823-0498
(727) 821-0088 fax
www.travelbase.com/destinations/st-pete/bayboro-inn

6 rooms, $65–110
full breakfast, non-smoking inside

Bayboro Inn and Hunt Room

THIS 1914 HOUSE ON the south edge of downtown St. Petersburg has been a boarding house and was a bank for a while. It underwent a renovation in 1994. Each of the rooms features a different decorative theme: Egyptian, Victorian, Renaissance, Art Deco, Key West, and Southwestern.

Vinoy House Bed & Breakfast
532 Beach Drive Northeast
St. Petersburg, Florida 33701
(727) 827-4855
(727) 550-9359 fax
reservations@vinoyhouseinn.com
www.vinoyhouseinn.com

6 rooms, $80–205
Continental breakfast, bicycles, game room with billiard table

THIS WAS THE HOME of Vinoy Hotel builder Aymer Vinoy Laughner and his wife, Stella. (See history notes in Renaissance Vinoy Resort description earlier in this chapter.) Perry Snell, a major developer in St. Petersburg's early years, built the house in 1910, and Laughner bought it in 1919.

Vinoy House Bed & Breakfast

The Florida International Museum
100 Second Street North
St. Petersburg, Florida 33701
(800) 777-9882

The Salvador Dali Museum
1000 Third Street South
St. Petersburg, Florida 33701
(813) 823-3767

The Museum of Fine Arts
255 Beach Drive Northeast
St. Petersburg, Florida 33701
(813) 896-2667

Tampa

Don Vincente de Ybor Historic Inn
1915 North Republica de Cuba/14th Street
Tampa, Florida 33605
(813) 241-4545
(813) 241-4646 Carlino's Restaurant

16 rooms, $100–200
full breakfast, restaurant, lounge

HISTORIC INNS AND BED & breakfasts have been conspicuously absent from my hometown of Tampa—until now. As this book heads to the printer, the sawdust is flying in Tampa's historic Ybor City.

Ybor often gets compared to New Orleans' French Quarter because of its similar architecture and nightlife. However, Ybor is not French. It was settled and populated by Spanish, Cuban, and Italian immigrants who came here to work in the cigar industry. Spaniard Vincente Martinez Ybor was a tobacco merchant from Cuba who opened the first cigar factory in Tampa in 1886 and developed the community that would become Ybor City. Two decades later, Ybor City had become the "cigar capital of the world."

As of this writing, historic renovator and Tampa native Jack Shiver is putting the finishing touches on the Don Vincente de Ybor Historic Inn. It is in the historic, two-story structure that was known for more than half a

Don Vincente de Ybor Hotel

century as the Gonzalez Medical Clinic. It had been constructed as an office building, pharmacy, and café in 1895, then converted into a mutual-aid clinic for cigar factory workers in 1903. Dr. Aurelio Gonzalez purchased the clinic in 1937, and it functioned in that capacity for another forty years before closing. Shiver bought the property in 1998 and is nearing the completion of a $2 million renovation. The inn is expected to be an elegant, sixteen-room bed & breakfast with a restaurant and lounge. The restaurant will be operated by popular local restaurateur Rita Carlino.

Anna Maria Island

Harrington House Beachfront Bed & Breakfast
5626 Gulf Drive
Holmes Beach, Anna Maria Island, Florida 34217
(941) 778-5444
(888) 828-5566
(941) 778-0527 fax
www.harringtonhouse.com

16 rooms, $129–239
full breakfast, bicycles, kayaks, beachfront, pool, non-smoking,
children over 12 welcome

SINCE I PREVIOUSLY VISITED the Harrington House while researching
Anna Maria Island for my 1996 book, *Visiting Small-Town Florida*, I noticed
that they have added "Beachfront" to their name. That was a smart move,
because elegant bed & breakfasts right on the beach are a rare find. This is
a gracious yet relaxed and comfortable place, as beach houses should be.
Think *The Big Chill* on the beach.

The three-story, coquina-masonry, cypress-framed main house was built
in 1925. It has seven rooms on the second and third floors. Most have
balconies with sweeping views of the sand and the gulf. Owners Jo Adele
and Frank Davis have expanded by adding adjacent houses. The 1940s
Spangler Beach House (south of the main house) has four rooms, and the
Davises recently added the Huth Beach House (a couple blocks north) with
four more rooms. Dr. Huth was the first doctor to reside on Anna Maria.

I stayed in the one-room cottage right next to the main house. It has a
queen-size bed with a fluffy, quilted, down comforter; a heart-shaped Jacuzzi
tub; and its own beach-facing deck and sliding glass door entrance. A gazebo
sits in the shade of Australian pines just outside the door. The beach and
the Harrington House pool are just a couple of steps beyond that. All the
amenities that a beach house should have are available for guests: sea kayaks,
beach-cruiser bikes, plus a lobby bookcase filled with paperbacks and videos
(the rooms have VCRs).

Seven-mile-long Anna Maria Island has been a favorite getaway for
west coast Floridians since the early 1900s. It is an uncrowded and unhurried
beach community, easily traversed on a bicycle. Despite its prime location
south of the entrance to Tampa Bay and just offshore from Bradenton, the

Harrington House

island has managed to fend off the high-rise condo and hotel invasion and has retained its quiet beach-town flavor for over one hundred years. Pioneer George Emerson Bean filed for homestead on the island in 1893. With the help of his sons, he built its first residence at the north end, near where the Rod and Reel Pier is now. Bean died in 1898, but his sons and their families continued to live and build on Anna Maria. In 1911, his son George Bean Jr. teamed up with John Roser, the German baker who invented the recipe for Fig Newtons, to form the Anna Maria Beach Company and began the first commercial development of the island.

There are no sea walls in front of the Harrington House. Sea oats, pine trees, and a favorable tide, which swirls around north Anna Maria's Bean Point at the entrance to Tampa Bay, fortify the wide, sandy beach.

A "Florida frog-strangler," or torrential thunderstorm, blew through on the afternoon that I arrived. As quickly as it came, it was gone—just in time for me to walk the beach and watch the sunset filter pink, green, and red through the last storm clouds out over the gulf. My breakfast the following morning was equally colorful and also delicious: banana pancakes dusted with powdered sugar and a side medley of strawberries, blueberries, cherries, honeydew melon, and cantaloupe.

CENTRAL

BRUCE HUNT

Chalet Suzanne, Lake Wales

McIntosh

MCINTOSH, HALFWAY BETWEEN OCALA and Gainesville, is a quiet little hamlet of giant, moss-filled oak trees and century-old Victorian homes. Its original settlers were citrus and cotton farmers whose fields surrounded the town. After the big freeze of 1895, the farmers switched to vegetables—watermelon, crookneck squash, cabbage, lettuce. I'm told that the old Gist House at Avenue H and Fifth Street was built with the revenues of a single season's crookneck squash crop. Another farmer grew iceberg lettuce exclusively for the ocean liner *Queen Mary* and shipped it by train to New York.

At the end of Avenue G is McIntosh's restored railroad depot. It was built in 1884 by the old Florida Southern Railroad and was scheduled to be torn down in 1974. In 1973, a group of townsfolk who felt the depot was a valuable landmark formed The Friends of McIntosh to try to save it. They came up with the idea of putting on a festival to raise the money. The following year, they held their first 1890s Festival. They had twenty-five vendors and drew about thirty-five hundred people. The festival has run every year since, on the third or fourth weekends in October. It now draws forty thousand people and features tours of McIntosh's historic homes, storytelling, a parade, over three hundred vendors, and all-day live entertainment.

The Merrily Bed and Breakfast
Avenue G and 6th Street
McIntosh, Florida 32664
(352) 591-1180

3 rooms (some with shared baths), $70
Continental breakfast, resident golden retriever

HUGE LIVE OAKS GRACE every yard in McIntosh, their Spanish moss–covered limbs spreading out over the tops of homes and across streets. Some have trunks as big around as small houses (and look as though Keebler elves live inside them). Two of the grandest are in the front yard and backyard of Margie Karow's Merrily Bed and Breakfast on the south side of Avenue G.

The Merrily is a yellow, two-story Folk Victorian with black shutters and a steeply pitched tin roof. W. E. Allen, McIntosh's first postmaster, built it in 1888. It has two upstairs rooms—one with a queen-size bed, the other a double bed—that share a bathroom. There is also a downstairs room with twin beds and its own bath.

Margie's yard is filled with ferns, flowers, and caladiums.

Ocala

THIS IS HORSE COUNTRY, rolling hills and pastures lined with endless white picket fences. Some of the fastest, most famous, and most expensive racehorses in the world are bred in the farms that surround Ocala. It's Florida's little piece of Kentucky.

Seven Sisters Inn
820 South East Fort King Street
Ocala, Florida 34471
(352) 867-1170
(800) 250-3496
(352) 867-5266 fax
www.7sistersinn.com

8 rooms, $95–185
full breakfast, afternoon tea, bicycles, one- and two-day Mystery Weekend packages, non-smoking inside, children over 12 welcome, handicap-accessible room

THE SEVEN SISTERS INN, located in Ocala's historic Fort King Street district, is one of Florida's best known and longest operating bed & breakfasts. The original main house is a classic, three-story Queen Anne Victorian. The Historic Ocala Preservation Society lists it as having been built around 1895, but the owners believe it was actually 1888. Insurance agency owner and secretary/treasurer of the Ocala Building and Loan Association Gordon S. Scott was the original owner. His family lived there for forty years. Norma and Jerry Johnson did a thorough restoration in 1985 and converted the house into a bed & breakfast. They named each of the (then) seven rooms after Norma and her siblings. Bonnie Morehardt and Ken Oden, former airline/commercial pilots, bought it in 1991 and added an eighth room.

The exterior is bright pink and trimmed in turquoise and lavender. A large, covered verandah with green and white awnings wraps around the front and sides of the first floor. A smaller, second-floor porch with awning sits over the front entry. Next to it, a front corner turret with bay windows houses Norma's Room, where I have my reservation.

Despite being the least expensive room, Norma's Room is very charming and cozy. The five-bay-window turret makes a perfect sitting area, complete with wicker chairs occupied by teddy bears. Norma's theme is roses. The room features rose wallpaper and silk roses on vines wrapped around the posts of

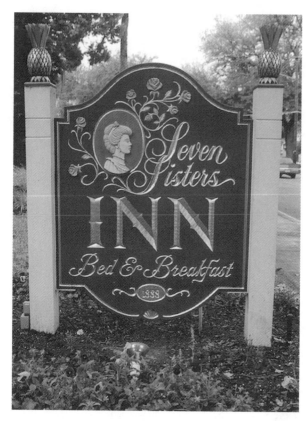

Seven Sisters

the queen-size four-poster bed. It even has a rose-patterned comforter. The twelve-foot ceilings are painted sky blue. My bathroom has all new Victorian-style fixtures—pedestal sink and claw-foot tub/shower with wraparound curtain. Across the hall is the library/television room. (My room has no TV, but most of the other rooms do.) The next room down the hall is Sylvia's, the honeymoon suite. The largest room, it has double doors, a fireplace surrounded with decorative tiles, a small crystal chandelier, and a king-size bed with a canopy of gathered drapes. Everything is peach and pink!

My favorite room (and in my opinion an even better honeymoon suite) is Lottie's Loft, which occupies the entire third-floor, built-out attic. Lottie's decor takes a dramatic departure from the other rooms' traditional Victorian surroundings. A narrow stairway leads up to a tropical oasis. Blue neon light bathes the room, which pays homage to the Caribbean and its colorful sea life. It feels like several rooms, with various nooks and crannies tucked beneath the steep gables and dormers. Glass bricks form a wave-shaped half-wall at the top of the stairs. A street lamp looks over Lottie's centerpiece—an elevated two-person Jacuzzi surrounded by black-and-white checked tile. Plastic palm trees, a beach ball, and a huge skylight complete the out-under-the-stars-in-Jamaica illusion. There's a queen-size bed in its own space beneath a dormer, plus two single beds hidden on the far side of the staircase. Each wall and ceiling panel is painted a different tropical hue—purple, yellow, turquoise, blue. A white wicker love seat (with more teddy bears) and chair make up a sitting area, and bright paintings with tropical fish and undersea panoramas hang on the walls. Two ceiling fans keep the breeze constant, which adds to the slightly surreal, outdoors feeling. Somebody had a lot of fun decorating this place.

I peeked into one more room, Scott's, which is downstairs. This one has a nautical theme and is also fully handicap accessible. A picture depicting the harbor in Mystic, Connecticut, sits over the fireplace.

I was sleeping soundly when sometime after midnight, a blazing thunderstorm blew through Ocala. My five bay windows lit up with each flash of lightning, and the thunder resonated in the house's hundred-year-old heart pine like a bass note pounded on a grand piano. It made quite a show, enough so that it was the main topic over breakfast the next morning (served promptly at nine).

I shared my breakfast table with a horse trainer from Texas who was in town to pick up a racing filly. We had bananas and strawberries in cream topped with shaved coconut, fresh-squeezed orange juice, homemade blueberry muffins, and (this is the first time I've ever had this for breakfast) chicken à la king.

Bonnie and Ken are expanding the inn. They have already renovated the two-story house (that fronts on S. E. 2nd Street) behind the main house. As of this writing, they are restoring the historic, circa-1890 Rheinauer House next door. It will be a perfect Queen Anne Victorian match to the main house. It originally belonged to Charles Rheinauer, Ocala's mayor in 1906.

Mount Dora

MOUNT DORA IS A storybook-picturesque town with tree-lined streets, Victorian streetlamps, and a multitude of parks, antiques shops, galleries, and restaurants. The "mount" is really a bluff that sits above Lake Dora. This little town bustles with activity. The list of festivals and events is lengthy: an antique boat show in March; an antique automobile tour in April; an annual art festival in February; and bicycle festivals in October and March.

Lakeside Inn

The entire month of December is one long Christmas festival with a lighted boat parade, street parades, and elaborate decorations and lighting throughout town.

Lakeside Inn
100 North Alexander Street
Mount Dora, Florida 32757
(352) 383-4101
(800) 556-5016
(352) 735-2642 fax
lakeside@magicnet.net
www.lakeside-inn.com

88 rooms, $95–215
restaurant, pool, tennis courts, boat dock

MOUNT DORA'S OLDEST STANDING structure, the Lakeside Inn, was built in 1883 and is listed on the National Register of Historic Places. Originally a ten-room hotel named the Alexander House, it was the joint project of key Mount Dora developers James Alexander, John MacDonald, and J. P. Donnelly. When they sold it in 1893, the name changed to Lake House. When it changed hands again in 1933, it became the Lakeside Inn. During the 1920s and the 1930s, the inn was the place to be in Mount Dora. One historical highlight of note: in the winter of 1930, Calvin Coolidge and his wife arrived at the inn for an extended sabbatical, following his just-completed term as president. During their stay at the inn, he dedicated the newly completed Gables and Terrace wings.

I stayed in a classically decorated, 1930s-era, second-floor room in the Gables wing. It overlooks the swimming pool and the courtyard that slopes down to Lake Dora.

James Barggren and Richard Dempsey bought the Lakeside Inn in 1992, and they have meticulously restored it to its 1920s–1930s heyday style. With tennis courts, a recently rebuilt pool and pool bar, and a boat dock on the lake, you'll never run out of activities. Perhaps the most enjoyable activity, though, is sitting in one of the rocking chairs on the main lodge's expansive verandah, sipping iced tea and soaking up the view across placid Lake Dora.

Darst Victorian Manor Bed & Breakfast

495 Old Highway 441
Mount Dora, Florida 32757
(352) 383-4050
(888) 533-2778
(352) 383-7653 fax
www.bbonline.com/fl/darstmanor

6 rooms, $125–220
full breakfast, children over 12 welcome, non-smoking, handicap-accessible room, modern replica of a grand, nineteenth-century Queen Anne Victorian

Winter Park

Park Plaza Hotel
307 Park Avenue South
Winter Park, Florida 32789
(800) 228-7220
(407) 647-1072
(407) 647-4081 fax
pkpho@mpinet.net
www.parkplazahotel.com

27 rooms and suites, $90–226
Continental breakfast in room, non-smoking, no young children,
adjacent to gourmet restaurant

THERE IS ANOTHER FAMOUS Park Avenue, and it's not in New York. As a community, Winter Park has done a terrific job of setting itself apart from mouse-crazed Orlando. Park Avenue is Winter Park's heart and main street. A beautiful, tree-filled park on one side and fine shops, boutiques, galleries, and restaurants on the other have made it an inviting place for decades.

The Park Plaza Hotel, at the south end of Park Avenue, fits in perfectly with its surroundings. This elegant boutique hotel was built in 1922. John and Cissie Spang purchased it in 1977 and upgraded it. Rich mahogany paneling and brass fixtures give the lobby an intimate warmth. The rooms are furnished with cushioned wicker and brass beds. French doors open onto balconies filled with potted plants and hanging ferns. Most guests enjoy breakfast on their balconies.

Lake Wales

Chalet Suzanne
3800 Chalet Suzanne Drive
Lake Wales, Florida 33853-7060
(863) 676-6011
(863) 676-1814 fax
(800) 433-6011
www.chaletsuzanne.com
airstrip UNICOM #s 122.8

30 rooms, $159–219

full breakfast, pool, antiques shop/museum, ceramic shop, soup cannery, vineyard, private airstrip, award-winning gourmet restaurant

CARL AND BERTHA HINSHAW had plans to develop a golf community in the rolling countryside near Lake Wales in the 1920s. Kraft Cheese Company president J. L. Kraft was to be a major partner, but bad timing worked against them. The collapse of the Florida real estate market, in the wake of the stock market crash of 1929 and the subsequent Great Depression, brought the project to a grinding halt. Then in 1931, Carl died of pneumonia. He was only forty-seven years old. Bertha, left with two young children, Carl Jr. and Suzanne, was determined to find a way to provide for her family. That same year, she opened Suzanne's Tavern. Soon she changed the name to Suzanne's Chalet and later to Chalet Suzanne.

Duncan Hines (yes, the cake-baking Duncan Hines), an early patron, helped put Chalet Suzanne on the map when he included it in his book *Adventures in Good Eating*. The first of many editions came out in the 1930s.

In the 1940s, a fire leveled the chalet. Carl Jr., returning from World War II, and Bertha rebuilt it using whatever materials and resources they had at their disposal. They relocated several buildings, including part of a horse stable and a chicken house, to construct what would evolve into today's dining hall, which overlooks Lake Suzanne.

Today the Hinshaw family continues to operate and expand Chalet Suzanne. All who have visited it and written about it proclaim it to be one of Florida's most enchanting and romantic places to stay and dine. My room was the Governor South, which sits above the dining hall. It shares with the Governor North room a wraparound patio, which is actually the dining hall roof. From the patio, I had a high, sweeping view of the lake. Dozens of turtles swam near the shore. Herons wandered along the banks, and a huge black swan paddled leisurely across the water. To my left, I could see one end of Chalet Suzanne's own lighted, twenty-five-hundred-foot grass airstrip. Private plane pilots from around the state have been flying in to Chalet Suzanne for dinner for years.

Chalet Suzanne is unlike any inn I've ever visited. More Swiss (or perhaps Swedish) village than inn, it felt as though I had stepped into a fairy tale— *Snow White*, *Wind in the Willows*, or *Alice's Adventures in Wonderland*. The grounds spread across seventy acres. Rambling brick walkways meander past fountains, gardens, and courtyards and wind through the colorful village, where each of the rooms, no two alike, has its own entrance. A tiny antiques shop/museum and a ceramics shop are nestled at the east end. Governor South is like no room I've ever stayed in. It is grottolike. The plaster walls and

Chalet Suzanne

ceiling are done in varying shades of peach and pink and seem almost free-formed. At the entryway, the ceiling is only about six and a half feet high; then it rises up to the center of the room. Likewise, the floor cants uphill from one side. It reminds me of a fun house room, where the slanting floor and ceiling give the illusion that a person is taller at one end of the room than the other. It is furnished with European antiques: a writing desk, dresser, and bedside tables. A round, king-size bed completes the nothing-is-square theme. If a large white rabbit and the Mad Hatter had popped out of the closet, I don't think I would have been completely surprised.

The night's stay includes breakfast, which is served from eight till eleven. There are no seating times. Just wander down whenever you like—which is nice, since that giant round bed and its twenty-two (I counted them) pillows of various shapes and sizes seem to conspire to make you sleep in. I had a choice of eggs Benedict or scrambled eggs and ham steak, with sweet, delicious Swedish pancakes (like miniature crepes) topped with Swedish lingonberry jam, plus sticky cinnamon buns. The gracious waiter happily brought seconds and thirds on the pancakes and buns.

Dinner at Chalet Suzanne (not included with the stay except in special packages) is a six-course, all-evening affair and is quite elegant (and quite expensive). Entrees include King Crab Thermidor, Maine Lobster Newburg, Filet Mignon, and Crab Sassé. The inn's gourmet meals are known worldwide, but perhaps better known are the soups. In 1956, the Hinshaws began canning their own soups. In 1973, NASA sent cans of Chalet Suzanne's Romaine soup to the moon on Apollo 15 as part of the astronaut's food supply. The "Moon Soup" has been on several missions since.

A string of adjectives comes to mind when I think of the Chalet Suzanne: storybook-like, romantic, eccentric, timeless, and simply wonderful. One more wonderful thing about Chalet Suzanne is its close proximity to what I consider to be Florida's most idyllic spot, Bok Tower Gardens.

The 205-foot-tall marble and coquina rock Bok Tower sits on top of one of the highest ridges in Florida and is easily visible for miles around. Bok Tower Gardens is a 157-acre sanctuary with a Technicolor assortment of flowers, trees, and plants and more than 120 wild bird species. The gardens and tower were the creation of magazine editor, author, and philanthropist Edward Bok and were built between 1922 and 1928. Live recitals play on the tower's fifty-seven-bell carillon from June through Labor Day and from December through April. Recordings of recitals play daily year-round.

Bok Tower Gardens
The Bok Tower Gardens Foundation
1151 Tower Boulevard
Lake Wales, Florida 33853-3412
(941)676-9412
(941)676-1408

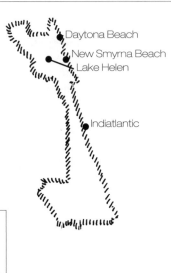

Daytona Beach

New Smyrna Beach

Lake Helen

Indiatlantic

CENTRAL
EAST

BRUCE HUNT

Clauser's Bed & Breakfast, Lake Helen

Daytona

Coquina Inn B & B

544 South Palmetto Avenue
Daytona Beach, Florida 32114
(904) 254-4969
(800) 805-7533
(904) 254-4969 fax

4 rooms, $80–110
full breakfast, non-smoking, no children, no alcoholic beverages,
two-story, 1912 stucco and coquina stone fascia house

Coquina Inn
Bed & Breakfast

The Villa

801 North Peninsula Drive
Daytona Beach, Florida 32118
(904) 248-2020 phone and fax
jim@thevillabb.com
www.thevillabb.com

4 rooms, $100–190
Continental breakfast, non-smoking, prefer no children (inquire),
pool, Rolls Royce available for special occasions

The Villa

THE VILLA IS AN immaculately restored Spanish Hacienda–style mansion that was built in 1929. The original owner, Bostonian Bartholomew J. Donnelley, would winter here in January and February, then close up the house the rest of the year. South Carolina bed & breakfast owner Jim Camp owns it today and has done a terrific job of renovating and decorating. The two-story, peach-colored house has arched entryways and windows, a red, barrel-tile roof, and overhanging balconies. A black, wrought-iron fence surrounds the lush one-and-a-quarter-acre grounds, which feature a variety of palm trees, a fountain, and a lawn that would make any greenskeeper proud. It sits four blocks inland from the beach—close enough to walk but just far enough away to be protected from traffic. The Villa is an excellent location for special occasions. Theywere readying it for a wedding and washing the Rolls Royce (which Jim keeps available for such events) when I was there.

The interior is decorated royally with artwork, antiques, and Oriental rugs. The upstairs Christopher Columbus and Queen Isabella Rooms have French doors that open onto balconies overlooking the pool. The King Juan Carlos Room opens onto a private rooftop terrace.

New Smyrna Beach

Riverview Hotel
103 Flagler Avenue
New Smyrna Beach, Florida 32169
(904) 945-7416
(800) 428-5858
(904) 423-8927 fax
rvhotel@aol.com
www.volusia.com/riverview/index.html

18 rooms (including 1 suite and 1 two-bedroom cottage), $80–200
Continental breakfast, bicycles, pool, restaurant, boat dock on
Intracoastal Waterway

THE RIVERVIEW HOTEL'S SHOCKING-pink paint scheme, with white trim
and burgundy canvas awnings, fits in perfectly at the west end of New Smyrna
Beach's colorful Flagler Avenue. The three-story, tin-roofed inn overlooks the
Intracoastal Waterway and the Musson Memorial Bridge, which leads to the
mainland.

Captain S. H. Barber built the structure in 1885. Barber tended the Coronado
Bridge, which was replaced by the Musson Memorial, and built what was then
a two-story hunting and fishing lodge, as well as his residence. In 1910, the
building was jacked up while a new lobby and dining room were constructed
beneath it. Originally named the Barber Hotel, it later became the Riverview.
It served as a youth hostel for a while in the 1970s. John Spang, owner of the
Park Plaza Hotel in Winter Park (see Chapter 4), bought and renovated it in
1984 and added the pool and a restaurant. Current owners Jim and Christa
Kelsey bought it in 1990.

No two of the eighteen rooms are exactly alike. The third-floor rooms
are my favorites, with their original, heart-pine, horizontal paneling and
ceilings. Its location, history, and decor give the Riverview a distinctive,
nineteenth-century, nautical atmosphere.

Riverview Hotel

Night Swan Intracoastal Bed & Breakfast

512 South Riverside Drive (at Anderson Street)
New Smyrna Beach, Florida 32168
(904) 423-4940
(800) 465-4261
(904) 427-2841 fax
nightswanb@aol.com
www.nightswan.com

16 rooms, $85–160
full breakfast, handicap accessible suite,
boat dock, non-smoking

CHUCK AND MARTHA NIGHSWONGER moved to New Smryna Beach from Utah in the mid-1980s. Both worked for Thiokol Propulsion, manufacturers of the space shuttle booster rockets. (Chuck still works for them at the NASA Space Center at Cape Kennedy.) While on their honeymoon in 1988, they stayed at bed & breakfasts in Pennsylvania and New York. That planted the seed for something they might want to do in the future. Two years later, they bought the house that, after a year and a half of renovation, would become the Night Swan.

A Philadelphia architect named Berger built the stately, three-story Colonial Revival main house in 1906. It was the Berger family's winter home.

Night Swan Intracoastal Bed & Breakfast

It has a hipped roof and full-width front and side porches, in keeping with the Colonial Revival style. There is also a second-floor porch connected to the River Breeze Suite, directly above the front entrance. The first floor exterior is pine clapboard, while the second-floor siding switches to cedar shake shingles—a combination found on many turn-of-the-century homes on this coast.

Martha tells me that she and Chuck have been able to meet people from every family that ever lived in the house except the Bergers. The Conelys lived there in the 1950s and returned to the Night Swan Bed & Breakfast for their fiftieth wedding anniversary. Mrs. Conely told Martha that the third floor had been a playroom when she lived there. It also had a cot that Mr. Conely used when he was "in the doghouse." The McGreevys and the Timmermans lived at the house in the 1950s and 1960s, respectively. The Williams family bought it in 1972. Chuck and Martha bought it from Mrs. Williams.

There are seven rooms in the main house. The second-floor Regatta Room has a king-size bed and an interesting bathroom configuration. Open the door and walk down two steps into a modernly appointed bathroom, which backs up against another bathroom. The two bathrooms were converted from an original, unfinished room that held the enclosed cistern for collecting rainwater. The River Breeze Suite, also on the second floor, has its own porch, furnished with a hammock, that overlooks the Indian River. It also has a step-down bathroom with a huge shower, all built from what had been a closet and window gable. In the Stinson Room (Stinson is Martha's grandmother's maiden name and Chuck's mother's maiden name), I found an old stand-up Sentinel Superhet Radio, which the couple brought from their previous home in Utah. The third floor rooms have the original cypress paneling and ceilings. I like the Captain's Suite, with its double-gable window and built-in window seat.

The Cygnet ("Baby Swan") House next door was built in 1910. Chuck and Martha finished renovating it in 1998. It also has seven rooms. It had been in the same family, the Brannons, since the 1970s. The downstairs Turnbull Suite (Andrew Turnbull was the founder of New Smyrna) converts to a meeting room. A terrific feature of the Turnbull is its enclosed front sunporch. An outside staircase leads to the upstairs rooms. The new renovation includes vaulted ceilings with large, exposed ceiling beams.

Behind the main house is the Carriage House, which was originally a horse stable. In the 1970s, the Williamses converted it into a two-story cottage for their oldest daughter. The Nighswongers removed the interior stairs, added a staircase on the exterior, and made it into two suites with their own private entrances. The upstairs suite has two bedrooms and a bath. The downstairs has a large bedroom, a Florida room, and a kitchenette.

The Nighswongers serve a full breakfast and have something that I think is a great idea—a sign-up sheet for when you would like your breakfast, anytime between 7:00 and 9:30 A.M.

Little River Inn
532 North Riverside Drive
New Smyrna Beach, FL 32168
(904) 424-0100
(888) 424-0102
little-river-inn@juno.com
www.little-river-inn.com

6 rooms, $79–159
full breakfast, tennis court, tandem bicycle, murder mystery weekends, 2 rooms with shared bath, handicap-accessible room, children over 12 welcome, non-smoking inside

---

THIS CIRCA-1883, THREE-story Southern plantation home overlooks the Indian River Lagoon from the mainland side, a few blocks from New Smyrna's historic Canal Street district. The two third-floor rooms occupy what was once the attic. The Lighthouse Room has a nautical theme with a

Little River Inn

king-size brass bed, brass lamps, and wood beams in the vaulted ceiling. During the restoration of this room, the leftover heart pine attic flooring was recycled and used as horizontal paneling. The pine's surface shows evidence of being sawn with a straight saw rather than a circular saw. The straight-saw cuts helped to date the house back to the 1880s. What makes this room my favorite is the distant view out the side window of the Ponce Inlet Lighthouse. The other third-floor room, the Garden Room, mirrors the Lighthouse Room's floor plan but is decorated with a more feminine touch. The pale blue Parisian Room, on the second floor, is the honeymoon suite. A hammock invites you to spend some lazy time on its second-floor porch.

Doug and Joyce MacLean have owned the Little River Inn since 1995. Joyce collects antique purses, and she has the best of her collection mounted in frames and displayed in the living room.

Somerset Bed & Breakfast

502 South Riverside Dr.
New Smyrna Beach, FL 32168
(904) 423-3839
(888) 700-1440
(904) 423-2286
somerset@ucnsb.net
www.somersetbb.com

4 rooms (3 rooms upstairs in main house and 1 Carriage House suite with kitchen and living room), $98–155
Continental breakfast, recently renovated, boat dock on the Intracoastal Waterway, on-premises massage therapist, bicycles

Lake Helen

Clauser's Bed & Breakfast
201 East Kicklighter Road
Lake Helen, Florida 32744
(904) 228-0310
(800) 220-0310
(904) 228-2337 fax
ClauserInn@totcon.com
www.clauserinn.com

8 rooms, $95–140
full breakfast, pub, non-smoking inside, children over 16 welcome,
Mystery Weekends ($350 per couple per room for two nights)

IT IS NOT BY accident I'm at Clauser's Bed & Breakfast on Halloween week-end. Less than a mile down County Road 4139 is the odd but quaint little community of Cassadaga, whose residents spend a good deal of their time communicating with the dead. I first happened upon Clauser's in 1996 while I was researching Cassadaga and Lake Helen for my book *Visiting Small-Town Florida*. When I saw it, I knew I would have to return on Halloween.

They were on a much-needed vacation when Tom and Marge Clauser first contemplated leaving their hectic jobs in Orlando and starting a bed & breakfast.

"We were staying at the Sweetwater Farms Bed & Breakfast in the Brandywine Valley in Pennsylvania," Marge explained. "Sitting on the back porch, overlooking a pasture of grazing sheep, deer were walking out of the woods and nibbling on the grass—Walt Disney could have created the scene. The innkeeper had just brought us two glasses of port and a plate of cheese. Tom turned to me and said, 'We could do this. You would be good at it.' And the seed was planted."

A few years later, while stopped at a general store in Cassadaga, they happened upon a horse saddle like one Tom had been searching for. The following weekend they returned, intent on buying the saddle, but it was gone. The storekeeper gave them directions to where they might catch up with the saddle's owner. Eventually they found him and bought it (it's now part of the decor in their Laredo Room). On the way back, they saw a hand-painted sign advertising a crafts show and took a detour up Kick-lighter Road to check it out. At the top of the hill stood their future home and bed & breakfast.

"It was rough looking. It wasn't even for sale. I called it a 'hound dog house' because you could look right underneath it and see where the hound dogs were lying," recalled Marge. "But the minute I saw it, I fell in love with it."

The Clausers left their phone number with the owners but didn't hold out much hope of hearing from them. Three months later—one day before closing on a parcel of land on which they had decided to build a bed & breakfast— they got a call from the owner of the old house.

On New Year's Day in 1990, Tom and Marge opened Clauser's Bed & Breakfast with only two guest rooms. Word of the charming country Victorian house and Marge's marvelous cooking spread fast. When they found that they were turning away twice as many customers as they were booking, the Clausers decided to expand. In 1994, they built a separate Carriage House behind the original house, with six more rooms and something out of the ordinary for a bed & breakfast: an English pub, which they call Sherlock's.

The Clausers have done an excellent job of restoring the original, three-story Victorian house. Outside, the broad, wraparound porch, filled with rocking chairs, invites you to sit and soak up the serenity. Inside, the front sitting room, dining room, and especially the kitchen are decorated to give the place a warm, country-home feeling. A gallery of pictures hangs on one wall, old family photos from both Marge's and Tom's families. One is of General George Armstrong Custer, Tom's great-great uncle.

During my stay, guests tended to gravitate toward the kitchen to sit around the kitchen table and chat, drink coffee, and munch on whatever wonderful concoction Marge may have baked that morning. Baking is Marge's therapy. For a while, she even ran a tea room in the main house. She also collects recipes and has written and published a cookbook, *Cooking Inn Style,* that has some of her most-requested recipes, such as Caramel Breakfast Rolls, Stuffed French Toast, and Breakfast Bread Pudding.

Breakfast is a big event at Clauser's. Ours began with a cup of apples, bananas, strawberries, and grapefruit. The main attraction was French toast stuffed with a filling of cream cheese and powdered sugar with grilled sausage on the side. Marge is a poetry fan. To entertain us during breakfast, she read a poem appropriate for the season, "When the Frost is on the Pun'kin" by James Whitcomb Riley.

I stayed in the Carriage House in the Cross Creek Room, named after Marjorie Kinnan Rawlings' home. It is decorated in old 1920s–1930s Florida Cracker style. The lap pine paneled walls are painted bright yellow and white. The queen-size main bed and a separate wicker daybed have colorful country quilts. An old schoolroom desk sits in one corner, and, of course, there is a copy of Rawlings' autobiography, *Cross Creek*, on the nightstand. Each of the

Clauser's

Carriage House rooms has its own screened porch. Out on mine, there was a collection of implements like those you might find at an old pioneer Florida home—a wooden surveyor's sexton, an old water pump, and rustic furniture.

Each of the eight rooms has its own theme. Marge explained, "For the Carriage House rooms, we took places where each of us had lived, or that were a part of our heritage, or that meant something special to us and built the themes around them. The Lancaster Room is done in Pennsylvania Dutch—that's Tom's heritage. The Windsor Room is English—we love England and both of us have some British ancestry. The Lexington is our red-white-and-blue Colonial American room. Charlevoix, our honeymooner's room, has a Jacuzzi tub and a fireplace. It's named for a town in upstate Michigan. The Laredo Room is our cowboy-theme room. We both love Western style, and this one's got it—log cabin walls, a horse trough bathtub, and Tom's saddle. Cross Creek is my Florida room. That old schoolhouse desk was mine from first grade."

The two rooms in the main house are named Peaches and Cream and Lilac and Lace and are decorated accordingly. My favorite of all of them is the Laredo Room. It's right out of an old Bonanza set. Horseshoes, a bullwhip, and a ten-gallon hat hang on the wall. It has wooden barrels for nightstands and a king-size bed frame made from logs to match the walls.

Clauser's address reads Lake Helen, but it's just as close to Cassadaga. The two communities are only about two miles apart. Lake Helen is a quaint town of about twenty-three hundred people, with large Spanish moss–filled oak trees and beautifully restored Victorian homes, such as the John Porter Mace home, "Edgewood," on Euclid Avenue. Henry DeLand founded the town in 1884 and named it and the town's picturesque lake after his daughter.

The tiny village of Cassadaga, all fifty-seven acres, has been designated a historic district on the National Register of Historic Places. All of the town's residents are spiritualists, mediums, or psychics. A century and a quarter ago, spiritualist George Colby claimed to have been given directions by his Indian spirit guide, Seneca, who instructed Colby to take a journey to Florida and build a community where other spiritualists could learn, live, and teach. In 1880, Colby found in wild central Florida what he claimed to have seen in his vision. Fourteen years later, a group from New York approached George Colby about organizing the Southern Cassadaga Spiritualist Camp Meeting Association. In January 1895, he deeded thirty-five acres of his property to the association, and the community of Cassadaga was born.

Cassadaga's narrow streets are lined mostly with cute, brightly painted, gingerbready cottages, although a few are a little creepy, obscured by over-grown vines and overhanging Spanish moss. All have a shingle hanging out front that typically reads, "Dr. or Reverend So-and-So, Certified or Registered Medium: Palmistry, Tarot, Spiritual Guidance. Readings by appoint-ment only." Depending on a particular psychic's best-developed abilities, he or she will divine what's in store for you in the future by reading tarot cards, your palm, or your aura. Some psychics may interpret your dreams or, in a longer session, do a past-life regression. Not your run-of-the-mill small town. You can see why I thought this would be an interesting place to stay on Halloween weekend.

Clauser's is listed on the National Register of Historic Places as the Ann C. Stevens House, built circa 1895 (although Tom and Marge suspect that it may have actually been built in the late 1880s). The property was part of George Colby's original homestead. He sold it to Stevens, a fellow spiritualist and farm owner from Michigan. Stevens Street in Cassadaga is named for her.

Despite Halloween, nothing supernatural happened to me while I visited Clauser's or Lake Helen or Cassadaga. However, in Cassadaga they were throwing a pretty good costume party. I was surprised not to see any ghosts, goblins, or ghouls. The best costumes I saw were a Tinkerbell and a Bozo the Clown. But I still had to ask Marge, "Are there any ghosts in the house?"

She hesitated a little before answering, then told me, "When we first started in this business, we didn't say anything, because we thought it might make the guests nervous. Now, after ten years, well, if they ask, I'll tell them about it. There is one room upstairs, Peaches and Cream, where I've had some guests tell me about some unusual things that have happened. One guest, who was in the room by herself, said she felt someone sit on the bed next to her and pat her on the knee. Sometimes items have been moved around in the house while no one was here. One morning I walked in here (the sitting room), and no one else had been in the house, and that teddy bear, which stays on that table, had moved right out to the middle of the floor. But the weirdest thing that I saw happened while my daughter-in-law and I were standing in the kitchen. I was talking about maybe needing to expand the house. This was before the Carriage House. I was saying that, if need be, we could knock this one kitchen wall down and build out to expand the room. While we were having this conversation, the candle holder that hangs on that wall began to swing back and forth, and it didn't stop! That freaked both of us out—we ran out of the room. Needless to say, I decided against knocking down that wall. In fact, once we found out that this is the oldest house in Lake Helen that has its original footprint—it's never been added to or taken away from—we decided never to expand the main house."

They have expanded outside the house, though. In addition to the Carriage House, Tom and Marge built a beautiful courtyard garden between the two buildings, with a gazebo and an outdoor hot tub. All indications are that the resident spirits are pleased with what the Clausers have done with the place.

Indialantic

Windemere Inn by the Sea

815 South Miramar Avenue
Indialantic, Florida 32903
(407) 728-9334
(800) 224-6853
www.windemereinn.com

9 rooms, $110–195
full breakfast, 4 rooms with Jacuzzis, Italianate Victorian reproduction house on the beach, country English decor

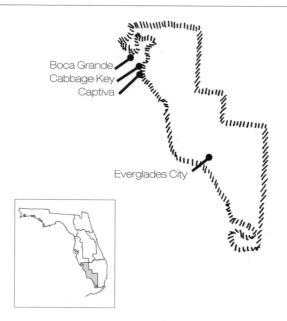

Boca Grande
Cabbage Key
Captiva

Everglades City

SOUTHWEST

BRUCE HUNT

Rod & Gun Club, Everglades City

Gasparilla Inn

Boca Grande

GENERATIONS OF FLORIDA FAMILIES have been coming to Boca Grande on Gasparilla Island for the better part of a century for its relaxed island atmosphere and its world-famous tarpon fishing. Gasparilla Island is accessible only by the privately owned toll bridge at its north end and by boat.

For most of the 1800s, the island's few inhabitants were transient—some Cuban mullet fishermen and a few rumrunners. Then, in 1885, phosphate was discovered mid-state up the Peace River from Charlotte Harbor. Suddenly, Gasparilla Island, at the mouth of Charlotte Harbor, became an important piece of property.

Albert Gilchrist, later Florida's twentieth governor, was the first to consider residential development here. In 1897, he purchased six hundred acres and platted half a dozen blocks just south of where downtown Boca Grande is today. It was Gilchrist who came up with the name Boca Grande (Spanish for "big mouth," referring to Boca Grande Pass at the mouth of Charlotte Harbor), but it was Boston fertilizer magnate Peter Bradley who brought the town to life. While Gilchrist was planning Boca Grande, Bradley was buying up phosphate mining properties along the Peace River. In 1899, Bradley combined his assets to form the American Agricultural Chemical Company. In 1907, he completed the Charlotte Harbor and Northern Railroad, with its terminus at Boca Grande, to replace the river barges that had been hauling his phosphate. Bradley traded company stock for Gilchrist's property and bought additional property around it. He laid out streets, built the railroad station, planted trees (including the beautiful banyans on Banyan Street between Gilchrist and Park Avenues), and began building homes. He also built the Gasparilla Inn.

Gasparilla Inn and Cottages
Palm Avenue
Boca Grande, Gasparilla Island, Florida 33921
(941) 964-2201

154 rooms in the main inn, 19 quadruplex cottages, $150–416 main inn open from December to June only, cottages open from November to June only, no credit cards, various meal plans depending on month, golf course, tennis courts, pool, restaurant

BOCA GRANDE'S MOST REGAL edifice was and still is the Gasparilla Inn. Constructed in 1911 and 1912, it opened in January 1913. Originally, the inn was a simple twenty-room hotel, but within one year of its opening, expansion was needed to accommodate its growing guest list.

The inn's owner, Bostonian Peter Bradley, hired father and son Frank and Karl Abbott, also from Boston, to manage the inn. For the dining room, the Abbotts shipped meat in from Boston and brought fresh produce and tanks of drinking water from Arcadia on Bradley's railroad. They imported their seasonal staff from high-class hotels in the Northeast. The Gasparilla Inn quickly became a very exclusive place for Boston socialites to vacation. It became so exclusive that the Abbotts began asking for social references before making a reservation. Names like DuPont, Drexel, and Eastman regularly filled the registry during its first decade and a half. However, by 1930, much of the inn's luster had faded. It had slipped into disrepair, and industrialist Barron G. Collier scooped up the bargain. He expanded the hotel, adding more rooms, a solarium, and the renovated front entrance that stands today.

Today the Gasparilla Inn is a classic resort in the tradition of the Barron Collier era, with a golf course, tennis courts, swimming pools, and grand dining halls. The three-story hotel is painted bright yellow with white trim and a burnt-orange shingled roof. Collier's two-story-tall, white columns guard the front entrance. The main hotel has 154 rooms. Nineteen additional quadruplex cottages, which can be opened up to accommodate families or groups, occupy several blocks in the surrounding neighborhood. Citrus trees, Australian pines, and towering palms grow throughout the grounds. The cottages are open from November to June, the main inn from December to June.

I stayed in one of the one-bedroom, one-bath cottage rooms. It was very spacious and had its own sunporch. When I opened the door to the porch, I recognized a wonderful aroma from my childhood—the smell of salt air–weathered wood. It was the smell of my grandmother's beach house on Indian Rocks Beach, where I spent much of my summers in the 1960s and 1970s.

The rooms in the main hotel are also surprisingly large, particularly for a hotel of its vintage. Charming and somewhat nostalgic, 1950s-style furnishings decorate the rooms' interiors. The yellow theme continues inside, accompanied by white and green trim. Three magnificent mural paintings hang on a wall in one of the dining rooms. Artist Cecilia Jonsson-Bisset painted two of the elaborate and vivid underwater scenes in 1985 and the third in 1995.

The hotel gets its name from the island that Boca Grande occupies. Gasparilla Island is synonymous with the mythical pirate Jose Gaspar, who reputedly adopted the island as his and his crew's headquarters and hideout. The story of ruthless pirate and notorious womanizer Jose Gaspar was told repeatedly by a crusty old Cuban fisherman known as Juan Gomez and also as Panther Key John. Actually, "old" is an understatement. Reportedly, Juan Gomez was 119 years old when he died in 1900.

It's likely that Gasparilla Island was really named after a group of Spanish priests who ran a mission in Charlotte Harbor. Old charts predating Gaspar's presumed lifetime show Gasparilla Pass as "Friar Gaspar Pass." Now most historians concur—Jose Gaspar was nothing more than the figment of Juan Gomez's imagination.

In 1918, the Charlotte Harbor and Northern Railroad released a publication that pieced together some of Gomez's anecdotes. They called it *The Gasparilla Story*. Most current historians think this is how the pirate story became widespread. The publication also contained sales advertisements for property owned by the railroad in Boca Grande, the terminus of its railway on Gasparilla Island. The sales effort turned out to be lackluster, but the romanticized story of Jose Gaspar became accepted as fact.

There is little doubt that real pirates did frequent this coast and probably visited Gasparilla Island in the 1700s. Pirate Henri Caesar, known as Black Caesar, made Sanibel Island his headquarters in the late eighteenth century.

Cabbage Key

Cabbage Key Inn and Restaurant

P.O. Box 200
Pineland, Florida 33945
(941) 283-2278

6 rooms in the inn, $89
7 cottages, $150–300
no air conditioning, accessible only by boat

FIRST, RENT A BOAT (unless you own one). That's the only way to get to Cabbage Key, a one-hundred-acre island in Pine Island Sound, between Cayo Costa and Pine Island.

I rented a nineteen-footer from Jensen's Marina on Captiva Island. From there, I motored north, following the directions on my chart to marker 60, then steered around the northeast side of the island to the dock and boathouse. A friendly dockmaster greeted me and politely explained that only overnight guests or patrons of the restaurant are allowed to come ashore. "The island is self-sufficient, you know, and our septic tank can only handle so many visitors," he explained. I assured him that I was there for the famous Cabbage Key cheeseburgers, and he welcomed me ashore with a smile. It is widely rumored that this place was the source of inspiration for Jimmy Buffett's "Cheeseburger in Paradise." I have heard the same rumor about the Le Select Bar and Grill in Gustavia on St. Barts in the Caribbean. Having sampled burgers from both places, all I can say is that Cabbage Key has the tastier burger. Jimmy's not telling.

It's a short, uphill walk from the dock to the "old house," now the inn and restaurant. The rustic, single-story pine home sits on top of a thirty-eight-foot-high Calusa Indian shell mound. Large, gracious oak trees shade the grounds around it. At the top of the hill, a big black Labrador retriever greeted me as if he were the host. Inside, the walls, ceilings, and doorways are wallpapered with autographed and dated one-dollar bills taped up by patrons. Of course, I had the requisite Cabbage Key cheeseburger, along with a slice of fresh key lime pie, the only dessert on the menu.

In 1929, Alan and Grace Rinehart, son and daughter-in-law of famous detective/mystery novelist Mary Roberts Rinehart, purchased the then-uninhabited island for only $2,500. The retreat that they built is now the Cabbage Key Inn and Restaurant, and it is a virtual island time capsule from the 1930s. The current owners, the Wells, bought the island in 1974.

Cabbage Key Inn

Accommodations are split between six rooms in the inn and seven rustic cottages tucked among the oaks and mangroves. A few have docks. I must emphasize the word "rustic" here. Most people who stay overnight on the island do so in the winter months, since the cabins don't have air conditioning. I have yet to stay overnight, but those who have tell me that once the restaurant crowd leaves, it is one of the most tranquil places on the planet.

Jensen's Marina
P.O. Box 191
Captiva Island, Florida 33924
(941) 472-5800

Captiva Island

DURING THE EIGHTEENTH AND early nineteenth centuries, the southwest coast of Florida was a prime pirate hideout. The barrier islands—Sanibel, Captiva, North Captiva, Cayo Costa (or Lacosta), and Gasparilla Island—provided protection from the rough gulf seas. The interior islands, Pine Island (the largest), Useppa, and Cabbage Key, along with numerous smaller islands, made ideal hiding places for both the pirates' ships and their plunder. Merchant vessels sailing up Florida's west coast headed for New Orleans had to pass right by these islands. British pirate Brewster "Bru" Baker worked these waters and is thought to have lived on Pine Island, across the sound from Captiva. (Rumor also says that he buried treasure there.) Henri Caesar, more widely known as Black Caesar, made his pirate's camp on Sanibel.

The mythical Jose Gaspar (see Boca Grande chapter, Gasparilla Hotel) was said to have ruled these waters in the early 1800s. According to legend, Captiva was so named because Gaspar used the island as a place to keep his captive women. One woman, refusing to become the bride of her pirate captor, was beheaded. Now her headless ghost haunts Captiva and nearby Useppa Island.

Early Spanish maps, which predate Gaspar's supposed reign by a couple of hundred years, show the island as "Cautiva," perhaps a reference to Calusa Indians held captive as slaves by Ponce de León during his second visit to this area in 1521.

Travel guides invariably mention the two islands of Sanibel and Captiva in the same breath. They're right next to each other, and you must drive through Sanibel to get to Captiva. However, they have dramatically different atmospheres. Once you cross the short bridge that spans Blind Pass, there is a noticeable shift in topography. Captiva is more wildly vegetated, more rustic, quieter, and less populated. It is almost Polynesian in its tropicalness. I didn't see any mowed-grass lawns. Dense flora hides most of the houses from sight. Trees hang over Captiva Drive, which runs the island's length.

'Tween Waters Inn

P.O. Box 249
Captiva Island, Florida 33924
(941) 472-5161
(800) 223-5865
www.tween-waters.com

137 rooms and suites (including 25 cottages), $105–550
pool, restaurant, boat dock

THE 'TWEEN WATERS INN sits roughly in the middle of the almost-four-mile-long island of Captiva, near its narrowest point between the Gulf of Mexico and Pine Island Sound. The inn has been a fixture here for three quarters of a century. Captiva's first homesteaders arrived in the late 1800s and early 1900s, long after the pirates had been vanquished. One of these homesteaders was Dr. J. Dickey from Bristol, Virginia. Dickey visited Captiva on a fishing trip in 1900, then returned permanently with his family in 1905. Since there were no schools on Captiva, along with his family Dickey brought a tutor, Miss Reba Fitzpatrick. He built a schoolhouse with living quarters for Miss Reba upstairs. Mr. and Mrs. Bowman Price, friends of the Dickeys from Bristol, purchased the schoolhouse and surrounding property in 1925. In 1931, they opened the 'Tween Waters Inn. Over the years, the Prices added cottages to accommodate new visitors who came down every winter. Cottages #97 through #106, along Captiva Drive on the gulf side, are some of these original cottages. In the late 1940s, the Prices floated Army barracks across the sound from Ft. Myers. These are units #111 through #114, next to the swimming pool and tennis courts. They also expanded the schoolhouse and converted it into the Old Captiva House Restaurant, now the centerpiece of the 'Tween Waters Inn property.

The 'Tween Waters Inn remained in the Price family (daughter Dorothy took over in 1962) until 1969, when a Kentucky development group purchased the property with the intention of building condominiums. Thankfully, their project never came to fruition. It sold again in 1976 to Rochester Resorts out of Rochester, New York. They're still the current owners. Rochester Resorts restored the old cottages and the Old Captiva House Restaurant. They also added five motel buildings, tennis courts, a marina, and a swimming pool. There are now 102 modern motel units and suites and 15 restored original cottages and duplexes.

'Tween Waters Inn

Some famous people made the 'Tween Waters their winter retreat. Anne Morrow Lindbergh, prolific author and wife of Charles Lindbergh, stayed here in the 1950s. She wrote one of her best known works, *Gift from the Sea,* while on Captiva. Jay Norwood "Ding" Darling, 1930s' political cartoonist and later head of the U. S. Biological Survey and founder of the National Wildlife Foundation, frequented the inn. He would rent two cottages—#103 to stay in and #105 to use as his studio.

My room was one of the modern motel units. It was spacious and comfortable, with a screened porch and a view through Australian pines and palm trees to the gulf. 'Tween Waters is a mix of the old and the new. The cottages are nicely restored and thoroughly charming. They have kitchenettes and screened porches with rocking chairs. Units #111 through #114 are nestled among coconut palms and are connected by a winding boardwalk. Although my room suited me fine, I will opt for one of the cottages on my next trip. My favorite is cottage #117, with a view of Buck Key across the Roosevelt Channel.

Like the rest of the island of Captiva, the 'Tween Waters property is generously landscaped with native flora: sea grapes, frangipani, crotons, spiny aloe, and all varieties of palm—sabal, coconut, royal, butterfly, and cabbage.

There are four restaurant choices at the 'Tween Waters Inn: Old Captiva House, Crow's Nest lounge, Canoe and Kayak Deli at the marina, and No-See-Um poolside bar and grill. My Sunday morning breakfast at the Old Captiva House was a feast and a bargain—an all-you-can-eat-for-$9 buffet of Belgian waffles, eggs benedict, French toast, omelets, bagels, muffins, and coffee cakes, with fresh-squeezed juices.

Captiva still retains much of its quiet and tropical ambiance from a century ago. The 'Tween Waters Inn does its part to maintain that atmosphere. Except for the Monday night "Nascrab" hermit crab races, don't expect this to be a rowdy place. Come to Captiva to get away from all that.

Captiva Island Inn/Bed & Breakfast
11509 Andy Rosse Lane
Captiva Island, Florida 33924
(941) 395-0882
(800) 454-9898
(941) 395-0862 fax
captivaislandinn@aol.com
www.captivaislandinn.com

4 cottages and 2 suites, $110–250
full breakfast at R. C. Otter's Restaurant across the street, bikes,
beach chairs, kitchens in all rooms

NEW OWNER SANDRA STILWELL recently purchased the Captiva Island Inn from Robert and Cathy DiGenero, who had done a superb job of restoring and updating these four historic island cottages one block from the beach. There are also two new suites in the front building. The cottages and suites are decorated in colorful Caribbean style, with Mexican tile floors, modern kitchens, front porches with hammocks, and air conditioning. Full breakfast at R. C. Otter's across the street is part of the package.

Everglades City

THERE ARE REALLY ONLY two seasons in the Everglades, mosquito and non-mosquito, which roughly coincide with the wet and dry seasons. The non-mosquito, or dry, season is from December through March, and while the Everglades is a hauntingly beautiful place year-round, this is by far the most pleasant time to visit.

Leave Naples behind and travel about forty miles down the Tamiami Trail through the Everglades. Turn south on SR 29, and cross the bridge at the Barron River. Everglades City is on the other side. It's a sleepy, little fishing community with a full-time population of fewer than four hundred. It's also one of two major entrances to the Everglades National Park.

This was industrialist Barron G. Collier's company town from the 1920s through the 1950s. It was an active shipping port for south Florida produce and commercial seafood. It was also the county seat. After Hurricane Donna ravaged the area in 1960, Collier pulled his interests out. The county seat moved to Naples, and Everglades City settled into the quaint fishing village it still is today. The homes in the center of town are mostly small, pastel-colored, clapboard cottages. All have at least one old boat up on blocks and in some state of disrepair in their side yards. Everglades City gained some notoriety in the 1970s when it was an active air-drop point for South and Central American marijuana runners.

Rod and Gun Club
2000 Riverside Drive
Everglades City, Florida 34139
(941) 695-2101

17 rooms, $65–95
no credit cards, pool, restaurant, boat dock

Rod & Gun Club

THE ROD AND GUN Club, alongside the Barron River, is an Everglades icon. The white, three-story, clapboard lodge with yellow and white awnings over windows and entrances hosted presidents and tycoons in its heyday. Present owner Pat Bowan has preserved the rustic lodge style that was the Rod and Gun Club's hallmark in the 1930s, '40s, and '50s, but you don't have to be a president to stay here now. Bowan no longer rents the rooms in the main lodge. Instead, the seventeen accommodations are in three cottage buildings on the north side of the property.

Everglades City founder W. S. Allen built the original building in 1850. When Allen passed away in 1889, George W. Storter bought the lodge, along with most of the surrounding property that comprised Everglades City, from Allen's estate. Storter paid only $800 for it. He enlarged the lodge to accommodate the hunters, sport fishermen, and yachting parties coming to the Everglades in increasing numbers each winter season. In 1922, Barron G. Collier took over. He operated it as a private club for his fellow industrial magnates and political dignitaries. Herbert Hoover, Franklin D. Roosevelt, Dwight Eisenhower, and Richard Nixon have all been guests at the Rod and Gun Club.

Framed newspaper articles and photographs of famous visitors cover the wall in the hallway that leads from the back door to the lobby. One photo shows a proud Robert Rand next to his trophy catch, a 7½-foot-long, 187-pound tarpon caught in March 1939. Another photo is of Dwight and Mamie Eisenhower. Dwight is wearing shorts and a scruffy fishing hat. The grin on his face and the long rack of fish behind him indicate that he must have had a big day.

The lobby is a trophy room. Ernest Hemingway would have felt right at home here. A five-foot-long sawfish bill, a gaping shark's jaw, a stretched alligator hide, deer and wild boar heads, and an assortment of game fish festoon the dark, wood-paneled walls. A pool table and an upright saloon piano occupy one end of the room. A large, open fireplace sits in the middle, though I can't imagine the weather getting cold enough to use it. The lobby opens into the dining room, which is an even bigger trophy room, with tarpon, barracuda, snook, lobster, and a giant, old sea turtle shell hanging on the wall. A stuffed raccoon looks over Pat Bowan's shoulder from its permanent perch behind the registration desk.

While I was talking to Pat, one of the guests came up to the desk and asked him, "If we get any phone calls this afternoon, would you just tell them we'll get back with them in a couple days?"

"There are no phones in the rooms, and that's the way our guests prefer it," Pat told me.

On the Banks of the Everglades Bed & Breakfast

201 West Broadway
Everglades City, Florida 34139
(941) 695-3151
(888) 431-1977
patty@banksoftheeverglades.com
www.banksoftheeverglades.com

13 rooms, $55–165
full breakfast, non-smoking, bicycles, shared baths in some rooms, well-behaved pets welcome with prior arrangement

On the Banks of
the Everglades

HOW WOULD YOU LIKE to have your breakfast served in the vault of a 1923 bank building? Or spend the night in the Mortgage Loan Department? This is one of the most unusual bed & breakfast applications of a historic building that I've seen.

On the Banks of the Everglades Bed & Breakfast occupies Barron Collier's old Bank of the Everglades, which ceased operations in 1962. Instead of trying to disguise the fact that it was a bank, father and daughter owners Bob Flick and Patty Richards have embraced it. They named the rooms for various bank departments: Small Business Loans, the Trust Room, the Checking Department. They have made the most of the old bank's flavor, giving it a museum-like feel. But don't worry: if the thought of having breakfast in a vault leaves you feeling claustrophobic, they will gladly serve your meal on their outside deck.

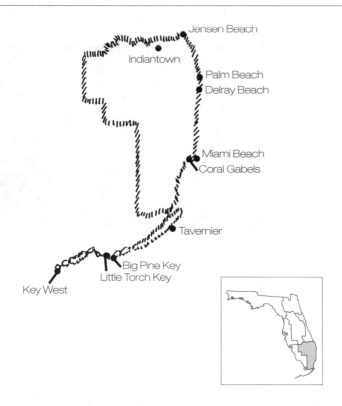

Jensen Beach

Indiantown

Palm Beach
Delray Beach

Miami Beach
Coral Gabels

Tavernier

Big Pine Key
Little Torch Key

Key West

SOUTHEAST

BRUCE HUNT

The beach at the Barnacle
Bed & Breakfast, Big Pine Key

Jensen Beach

Hutchinson Inn Seaside Resort
9750 South Ocean Drive (A1A)
Jensen Beach, Florida 34957
(561) 229-2000
(800) 909-4204
(561) 229-8875 fax
www.hutchinsoninn.com

21 rooms (1- and 2-bedroom suites with kitchens), $80–225
full breakfast, pool, tennis courts, beach, non-smoking,
resident English bulldog, Emily

Indiantown

Seminole Country Inn
P.O. Box 1818
15885 South West Warfield Boulevard
Indiantown, Florida 34956
(561) 598-3777
(888) 394-3777
www.bbonline.com/fl/seminole

25 rooms, $75–95
restaurant, pool

EXACTLY HALFWAY DOWN THE long, lonely stretch of Highway 710, between Okeechobee and West Palm Beach, lies Indiantown. The craziness of I-95 and Florida's "Gold Coast" is only forty minutes southeast, but it might as well be a thousand miles away. This is quiet agricultural country—mostly citrus groves and cattle pastures.

Indiantown's landmark structure is the Seminole Country Inn, and its history is integral with the town's. Seminole Indians settled here and operated a trading post in the early 1800s. Citrus growers and cattle ranchers had moved into the area by the 1890s. In 1913, the Army Corps of Engineers began building the St. Lucie Canal to connect the St. Lucie River (and its outlet to the Atlantic Ocean) with Lake Okeechobee. The canal passed just south of Indiantown, which made it an even more strategic trading location. Baltimore banker and president of what would later become the Seaboard Coastline

Seminole
Country Inn

Railroad, Soloman Davies Warfield, saw great potential in Indiantown as a major southern railway terminus. Around 1920, he bought several large tracts of land. He graded roads, built a train depot and a school, and had plans drawn up for a hotel. Construction on the Seminole Country Inn began in 1925, and it opened with considerable fanfare in 1926. Sadly, only seven months after the inn's opening, Soloman Warfield died, and so did his plans for converting Indiantown into a major rail hub.

An interesting piece of trivia—the hostess for the hotel's 1926 grand opening was Warfield's niece, Wallis Warfield Simpson. Ten years later, she would marry the Duke of Windsor, who passed up the opportunity to be king in order to marry her. The inn's two largest rooms are named for the duke and duchess.

The Seminole Country Inn sold several times over the decades. Homer Wall purchased it in 1974 and renovated it in 1975. He sold it and bought it back three times between then and 1993, when his daughter and current owner, Jonnie Williams, bought it. Jonnie invested roughly $750,000 to restore the inn and upgrade the grounds—quite a leap from the $66,000 it cost to build the inn in 1926. The inn maintains its original character and Spanish Mission–style architecture, with parapeted facades on the wings and barrel-tile roof over the central lobby. The dining room and lobby ceilings and walls, original to the structure, are made from pecky cypress harvested from the Allapattah Flats, a lowland bog that spreads out north of Indiantown. There is a large swimming pool, and the reception desk will arrange activities for guests, such as horseback trail riding, fishing on Lake Okeechobee, and touring the nearby Barley Barber Swamp. Oh, yes—Jonnie has made the Seminole Country Inn's restaurant famous for its Florida Cracker cuisine.

Palm Beach

THE ROOM RATES YOU see here are not misprints. It is estimated that among Palm Beach's winter residents are those who control fully ten percent of the world's wealth. America's "royalty" has been wintering here for a century. Donald Trump, the Kennedys, and descendants of DuPonts, Vanderbilts, and Rockefellers all have homes here. This tiny tendril of land (less than five square miles) along the Atlantic coast contains the most expensive real estate in Florida (probably in the United States), and its three-and-a-half-block long Worth Avenue must surely have the most expensive shopping in the country. I walked into one store that had a rack of several hundred identical leather belts—priced at $495 each. They also had a pair of tennis shoes for $1,875. There is, of course, a Tiffany & Co., a Cartier, a Gucci, and a Saks Fifth Avenue, plus an assortment of chic boutiques with unpronounceable names that all advertise locations in Paris, London, or Rome.

Ironically, this was no more than a backwoods hamlet with a dozen or so wooden shacks until Henry Flagler came along in 1893. (See next entry, The Breakers, and A Tale of Two Henrys for more information.)

The Breakers
1 South County Road
Palm Beach, Florida 33484
(561) 655-6611
(800) 833-3141
www.thebreakers.com

569 rooms (including 45 suites), $250–5850
pools, restaurants, tennis courts, health facilities, golf course

WHETHER YOU LOVE WHAT he did for Florida or despise what he did to it, you cannot help but be astounded by what Henry Flagler accomplished from one end of Florida's east coast to the other (see the Introduction for A Tale of Two Henrys). Perhaps more than any other city Flagler helped develop, Palm Beach truly achieved what he had envisioned.

Flagler first visited Palm Beach around 1890. At that time, there were only a few Cracker shacks along Lake Worth (which is actually a bay with an inlet from the Atlantic Ocean). In 1893, he returned and bought some property from Robert McCormick, one of the area's first settlers. When word leaked out that Flagler had bought there, property values skyrocketed. In May 1893, his crews began construction on the Royal Poinciana Hotel on the eastern shore of Lake

The Breakers

Worth. Amazingly, they finished this enormous, 540-room hotel in only ten months! (Later additions would bring the room count up to 1,100.) At its completion, it was the largest wooden hotel in the world.

Flagler had extended his railroad to Palm Beach as well. Just as he had done in St. Augustine, he quickly turned Palm Beach into a popular resort for the affluent. A staff of fourteen hundred catered to lodgers' every need. There were tennis courts, croquet lawns, a golf course, and a mule-drawn trolley that shuttled guests to the Atlantic Ocean beach less than half a mile away.

The beach turned out to be one of the area's biggest attractions, and that prompted Flagler to build a smaller, simpler hotel around an existing house right on the beach. He opened the Palm Beach Inn in 1896. It was so popular that within two years it had to be enlarged. Everyone wanted to stay "down by the breakers." When he remodeled and added on again in 1901, Flagler decided to make the colloquialism official and changed the name to The Breakers.

Two years later, during the construction of yet another wing, The Breakers caught fire and burned to the ground. Thirteen months after the fire, Flagler, true to form, rebuilt it. It was grander and even more palatial than before. The new Breakers had 425 rooms, a beachfront cabana with a saltwater swimming pool, and a fishing pier, plus seven individual cottages strung along the beach north of the main hotel.

On May 20, 1913, eighty-three-year-old Henry Flagler passed away at his cottage, which he had named the Nautilus, just up the beach from The Breakers. Mary Lily, his third wife, inherited most of his estate, including The Breakers and the Royal Poinciana Hotel. When Mary died in 1917, her family, the Kenans of Wilmington, North Carolina, took over operation of The Breakers and the Royal Poinciana.

On the afternoon of March 18, 1925, another fire broke out. Some speculate that a hair curling iron (a recent invention) started the blaze. It ignited in the south wing and rapidly leaped through the rest of the hotel, pushed by strong offshore winds. Amazingly, there were no fatalities, perhaps because in the afternoon most of the patrons were out on the beach. Photographs of the tragedy show black smoke billowing thousands of feet into the air. By nightfall, only the brick chimneys were still standing.

William Kenan Jr., Mary's brother and president of the Florida East Coast Hotel Company (which owned all the Flagler hotels), vowed, in the Henry Flagler tradition, to rebuild bigger and better and to have the new hotel completed in time for the following year's season. He kept his promise, borrowing some of the ideas that Henry Flagler had put to use in St. Augustine. The new Breakers would be built from concrete, not wood, and the architecture would reflect a European style.

Kenan hired the New York architectural firm of Schultze and Weaver, which a decade later would design the Waldorf-Astoria. Leonard Schultze chose to pattern the hotel's front entryway after Rome's twin-towered Villa Medici. He also modeled the fountain in the center of the circular drive after one of the fountains in Boboli Gardens in Florence. This set the tone for the new Breakers' Italian Renaissance architectural style.

Turner Construction Company, also from New York, started building the foundation in January 1926. The company opened a spur railroad track directly to the construction site to bring in some thirteen hundred carloads of stone, cement, brick, tile, lumber, and steel reinforcing. Twelve hundred workers lived on the premises and labored around the clock. Seventy-two artists from Italy painted murals on the lobby ceiling. Despite a July hurricane, the eye of which hit land only a dozen miles north of the construction site, the new Breakers opened four days after Christmas that same year. It was seven stories tall—eight if you included the penthouse or ten if you also included the towers. It had 425 rooms and cost $7 million.

The magnificent Royal Poinciana Hotel was dismantled in 1935, leaving The Breakers as the sole Flagler hotel in Palm Beach. Today's Breakers is essentially the same hotel that opened just before New Year's Eve in 1926. The North Carolina Kenans still own and operate it. There have been some changes along the way, however. From 1942 to 1944, the U.S. Army requisitioned The Breakers and converted it into the Ream General Hospital for wounded World War II soldiers. In the 1960s, a new wing with 150 rooms was added. Since Palm Beach had become a year-round destination, air conditioning was added in the 1970s. The biggest change has been a thorough, $75-million renovation that spanned 1990 to 1995. No detail was left untouched. Even the lobby and dining hall ceiling paintings were restored.

A long, straight driveway leads through the gates off South County Road, past immaculately manicured golf greens and through lushly landscaped grounds with acres of brilliant flowers. The Boboli-copy fountain, with its four water nymphs supporting the lower bowl, is the centerpiece of the circular drive in front of the entrance. A grand portico, with massive double columns holding up three ornate front arches and four side arches, shades the front entrance. Inside, the lobby has towering ceilings, more columns, and more arches. Eight, huge crystal chandeliers hang along the length of the arched ceiling beneath the paintings. It resembles a museum—or perhaps the Sistine Chapel or St. Peter's Cathedral—more than a hotel lobby. Even Michelangelo would be very impressed.

For the lobby, the architects drew inspiration from another sixteenth-century Italian structure, the Great Hall of the Palazzo Carega in Genoa. Ten-foot-long silk and wool tapestries, which Dr. Owen Kenan, Mary Flagler's cousin, brought over from France at the start of World War I, hang on the walls. As an interesting aside, Dr. Kenan returned from that trip on the ocean liner Lusitania in 1915, when it was attacked and sunk by German U-boats. He was one of the few survivors. Apparently he had shipped the tapestries by another means.

The Mediterranean and Venetian Ballrooms and the Florentine and Circle Dining Rooms are equally as impressive as the lobby. The Circle Dining Room has a thirty-foot-high, domed ceiling with a circular skylight, as well as oval murals that depict sixteenth-century Italian panoramic landscapes. The Venetian Ballroom was added in 1969.

The Breakers' 140-acre grounds contain beautiful gardens, more than four miles of hedges, and a wide variety of palm trees. Some of the palms are more than a century old, and one, a Canary Island date palm, is thought to be among the oldest palm trees in North America. The Pine Walk, a sidewalk that's nearly a quarter mile long and is lined with Australian pines and palm trees, leads to Whitehall on Lake Worth. Whitehall was once Henry and Mary Flagler's home and is now the Flagler Museum.

With its over six hundred rooms and suites and richly decorated formal lobby and dining halls, The Breakers may be as close as we can come to an American castle. Certainly the ancestors of Palm Beach's affluent residents are as close as we will come to American royalty.

Brazilian Court Hotel

301 Australian Avenue
Palm Beach, Florida 33480
(561) 655-7740
(800) 552-0335
(561) 655-0801 fax
info@braziliancourt.com
www.braziliancourt.com

103 total accommodations (including 11 junior suites,
27 1-bedroom suites, 8 2-bedroom suites, 2 corporate suites, and
3 penthouse suites), $140–775
pool, gourmet restaurant

THE BRAZILIAN COURT UNOBTRUSIVELY occupies an entire block between Australian and Brazilian Avenues in a quiet neighborhood three blocks west of the Atlantic Ocean and three blocks north of ritzy Worth Avenue. It looks very much like a Spanish hacienda, with its red barrel-tile roof, yellow stucco walls, and two open-air courtyards. This quietly elegant, two-story (three-story with the penthouse suites) hotel has catered to Palm Beach regulars since it opened in 1926. That was what New York architect Rosario Candela had in mind when he designed it, and today's iteration holds very true to his concept.

Brazilian Court Hotel

The "B. C." has had a variety of owners throughout its life. Following Florida's real estate bust in the early 1930s, it sold at auction for a paltry $125,000 to the Mulford Realty Company, which made some additions, including the third-floor penthouse suites. It sold again in 1963, 1978, and 1984, when it underwent an $8-million restoration.

The current owner, Abraham Gosman, purchased it in 1995 and has remodeled again. The hotel's entire interior has been redone; kitchenettes have even been added in every one of the 103 rooms. Impressive original artwork hangs in every hallway. One upper-floor wing features all Cubist art. Picasso would feel right at home. Gosman also added a fitness center and the much-touted Chancellor Grille Room Restaurant, where diners can observe the chefs at work in the open kitchen. At the same time, Gosman has maintained the original cultured but comfortable ambiance of the 1920s' Brazilian Court.

I stayed for one night in a second-floor, west-wing room that overlooks the pool through a panoramic window. In the distance, I could see the tops of the twin Trump Towers, a constant reminder that I was in a city where the median annual income probably equals the gross national product of some small countries. The room was very elegant without being ostentatious. Many of the Brazilian Court's clientele stay for a month, or two, or three. I could see that this is not only a wonderful place to stay, it would also be a wonderful place to live. Every conceivable amenity is available. The kitchenette's refrigerator is fully stocked with all kinds of snacks and beverages, including four different wines. There is even aloe gel for sunburn and a Fuji disposable camera! There's almost no need to step out the door, so I didn't. I ordered dinner from room service.

Four different menus cover twenty-four hours of room service. If you wake up ravenous at 3:00 A.M., no problem. Order a grilled ham-and-cheese or BLT, a Caesar salad, Norwegian smoked salmon, or Brazilian gourmet pizza. If you're craving chocolate, order the triple-chocolate cake; if not, the Key lime pie. I had dinner (at a reasonable hour), and my only difficulty was choosing which entrée to order. Did I want the Herbed Horseradish Seared Rack of Colorado Lamb or the Sesame Swordfish in Honey Teriyaki? I finally picked the Sea Bass Encrusted with Yukon Golden Potatoes. It came drizzled with a shallot fondue and white truffle oil vinaigrette and was served with steamed baby zucchini and carrots on the side. I also ordered the chilled lobster bisque and a jumbo shrimp cocktail that came with a marvelous salsa made from mangoes, tomatoes, cilantro, and grapefruit. It was all spectacular—no, make that life-reaffirming! Oh, yes, and Grand Marnier Crème Brûlée for dessert. I could get used to this.

The Brazilian Court gives new meaning to the rating Five Star. The staff is exceedingly courteous and accommodating. The food is outstanding. The tropical landscaped, open-air courtyards are inviting and romantic. This is as fine as it gets.

The Chesterfield Hotel
363 Cocoanut Row
Palm Beach, Florida 33484
(561) 659-5800
(800) 243-7871
(561) 659-6707 fax
chesterpb@aol.com
www.redcarnationhotels.com/chest_palm/index.htm

43 rooms and 11 suites, $89–1,500
pool, gourmet restaurant

THE SPANISH-MEDITERRANEAN revival–style Chesterfield Hotel blends discreetly into a residential neighborhood that borders Worth Avenue (a two-block walk south). There is no grand, circular drive leading to an entrance with fountains, just a simple canopied doorway. The understated exterior hides an intimate and luxurious boutique hotel. This is not the kind of place that you find splashed across the advertising pages of travel magazines. Instead, you might hear about it from an acquaintance who "travels in the right circles." I happened across it by accident while taking a walk through the neighborhood.

When it opened in 1926 as the Lido-Venice Hotel, it was touted for its fine restaurant as much as for its accommodations. Two years later, the name changed to the Vineta Hotel (and the Vineta Dining Room) and remained so for fifty years. Additions were made concurrent with changes in ownership in the 1930s, '40s, and '60s.

In 1977, new owners Leslie Raul and Francesca Eszterhazy renamed it the Royal Park, and for a while the hotel and restaurant reflected their Hungarian heritage. Jeno and Anna Flohr purchased it in 1980 and converted it into condominiums. In 1985, Lanny Horowitz and Carl Sax bought it, performed a $5-million restoration, and renamed it once again to the Palm Court. Now it was a combination condominiums/hotel and restaurant.

In 1989, the Tollman-Hundley Hotel Group of Great Britain bought the hotel. One more time the name changed. The Chesterfield is named after another of their properties in London that's named for the Fourth Earl of Chesterfield, Philip Dormer Stanhope, the sixteenth-century English statesman and

The Chesterfield Hotel

witty author. The Tollman-Hundley group performed additional renovation and gave the Chesterfield its decidedly British atmosphere. Currently it is part of the Red Carnation Hotel Collection, which owns six hotels, five of them in London.

The Chesterfield stakes its word-of-mouth reputation on attention to detail in its amenities and on relief from the attention of the outside world for those of its guests who require it. It has been a private enclave for Oscar de la Renta, Catherine Deneuve, Margaret Thatcher, Tony Bennett, Eartha Kitt, and Andy Rooney, to name just a few.

Throughout its history of multiple owners, this hotel has consistently maintained a fine gourmet restaurant. The Chesterfield carries on that tradition today in the Leopard Lounge and Supper Club, a lavish dining room with hand-painted Lino Mario ceilings. It has also become one of Palm Beach's favorite nightspots.

Delray Beach

The Colony Hotel
525 East Atlantic Avenue
P.O. Box 970
Delray Beach, Florida 33447
(561) 276-4123
(561) 276-0123 fax
info-fla@thecolonyhotel.com
www.thecolonyhotel.com

66 rooms, $69–270
open from November–April only, full breakfast, beachfront cabana
club with pool, restaurant

IN THE LATE 1980S, the citizens of Delray Beach decided that their downtown needed some help. The first step was to restore three historical buildings just off East Atlantic Avenue: the old Delray Beach High School building, the 1926 Crest Theatre, and the 1913 Cornell Museum. They accomplished these renovations in 1991, and this initiated the momentum to restore the surrounding area. Throughout the 1990s, East Atlantic Avenue, Delray's main street, along with the Pineapple Grove Historic and Arts District just north of the old schoolhouse, were completely revitalized. East Atlantic's new sidewalks, benches, and streetlights made it pedestrian friendly. Now, lined with restaurants, sidewalk cafés, shops, and galleries, it is the day-and-night hot spot for the area. Four times a year—in May, June, October, and December—the area hosts the very popular "Art and Jazz on the Avenue." Right in the middle of all the action is the Colony Hotel.

The Colony is Delray Beach's oldest hotel, built in 1926 by hotelier Albert Repp from Glassboro, New Jersey. Its stucco exterior, arched entryways, and red barrel-tile, low-hipped roof are typical of the Spanish/Mediterranean Revival style that Addison Mizner made so popular in this region during Florida's 1920s' land boom. Martin Luther Hampton, an associate of Mizner's, designed it. Not so typical are the red domes that cap the Colony's twin cupola towers, which rise behind the lobby, and the second-floor aerial cross-walk that leads to the staff quarters/carriage house behind the hotel.

There are some interesting features inside too. In a room off the east end of the lobby, a latch in the hardwood pine floor opens a hatch to reveal a stair-case. Was this a hiding place for liquor during Prohibition? Who knows? Now it is the Colony's wine cellar—a genuine cellar, something rarely found in

The Colony Hotel

Florida. A careful walk down the steep steps leads into a ten-by-fifteen-foot room with low ceilings. Cases of wine are stacked five feet high against all four walls. It even has its own dedicated temperature control system.

Another fascinating item (I haven't seen one of these in thirty years) is the old Otis manually operated elevator—the kind with a hand-closed metal gate and a mesh-reinforced glass door. "Going up!" The Colony doesn't employ a full-time elevator operator; usually one of the desk clerks will run it for you.

In 1935, the Boughton family bought the Colony, and they have owned and operated it since. Jestena Boughton is in charge these days. In 1988, she oversaw the refurbishment of the hotel. She also owns another Colony Hotel in Kennebunkport, Maine. That one was built in 1914, and the Boughtons bought it in 1948. The Kennebunkport Colony is open from mid-May until mid-October, and the Delray Beach Colony is open from November through April. Much of the staff works for both hotels, traveling back and forth during the season change. Apparently many of their clientele do the same. The Colony has a loyal following of regular guests who return year in and year out.

The lobby has a tropical Casablanca ambiance to it—carpet runners over terrazzo floors, large potted palms and ferns, antique wicker furniture, iron chandeliers from the 1920s. Two huge, semi-opaque skylights bathe the room in diffused light. Gorgeous black-and-white landscape photographs by Clyde Butcher hang on the lobby and hallway walls. Benny Goodman and Duke Ellington tunes float continuously through the lobby and out the front door. A piano player performs during happy hour in the shade of the arched front porch.

I stayed in the Seagrape Room, cheerfully done in peach with white trim, with bright, Florida-scene watercolors on the walls. It is a third-floor double room—king-size bed in one room and two double beds in the other, separated by the bathroom. Many of the door, window, and bath fixtures are original, as is the tile work in the bathroom.

The room rate includes breakfast, and it's only $11 if you're not a guest. Breakfast is served in the spacious dining hall, which seats 160. I had the pancakes with fresh Maine blueberries and Vermont maple syrup, grilled ham, muffins (with more fresh Maine blueberries), and fresh-squeezed orange juice. It was delicious.

An easy six-block stroll takes you to the beach, but you might as well hop the Colony's shuttle, which takes guests to their private beach cabana—complete with saltwater pool, lunch grille, and sunning deck.

My girlfriend, Loretta, and I were there in February—the height of "snow-bird" season—and the traffic reflected it. Fortunately, once I parked the car (parking is at a premium in Delray Beach, but the Colony has plenty of space in its private lot behind the hotel), getting around on foot was easy. One evening, we met friends Doug and Terrie for dinner at Louie Louie Too, a restaurant two blocks west of the Colony that merits mention. My angel-hair pasta with basil, tomato, and garlic and served with sautéed crab cakes was superb.

Louie Louie Too Restaurant
201 East Atlantic Avenue
Delray Beach, Florida 33447
(561) 276-3600

Miami Beach

South Miami Beach Resurrected

SOUTH MIAMI BEACH'S MYRIAD cultures contrast sharply but manage to coexist like parallel universes. Elder Jewish retirees—some in Orthodox dress and chatting in Yiddish—share the sidewalks with young Latin, European, and even some American yuppies, who in turn share them with younger roller blading models and model-wannabees. Their backdrop is a tropical pastel-by-day and neon-by-night collage of Art Deco architecture, retro-futuristic in a Flash Gordon kind of way. The most exotic German and Italian automobiles cruise Ocean Drive at a snail's pace. Those roller bladers zigzag around them

and down the sidewalks at triple their speed. When someone gets around
to making a noncartoon movie version of *The Jetsons,* it will no doubt be
filmed here.

At times, Ocean Drive looks like a giant outdoor fashion runway. It is bright,
bustling, alive, and sometimes outlandish. To tell you the truth, it can be so
crowded, noisy, and flashy that, after twenty-four hours of it, I'm ready to
leave. Today's Ocean Drive beats the heck out of what it used to be, though.

What had decayed into a poor and eventually run-down, retiree neighborhood in the 1970s evolved into a terrible, drug-dealing war zone in the
early 1980s. Who could ever imagine that this place would be the vibrant
community and the cultural and artistic crossroads that it now is? Well,
Barbara Capitman did.

In 1976, the ever-myopic city of Miami passed a redevelopment plan to flat-
ten everything south of 6th Street, the very southern tip of south Miami Beach.
The rest would not be far behind. Towering high-rises separated by canals was
the new concept—the city's idea of a modern version of Venice perhaps?
Thousands of low-income retirees would have been displaced. They may not
have been young, but they still knew how to protest. The retirees managed to
stave off the bulldozers long enough for Barbara Capitman to come along.

Capitman, a New York interior design journalist and magazine editor,
immersed herself in the cause of saving south Miami Beach, some say to fill a
void following her husband's recent death. At a cocktail party following an
American Society of Interior Designers meeting in 1976, she and designer
Leonard Horowitz concocted the idea of the Miami Design Preservation
League. They shared a disdain for the latest direction of some of Miami's
development—monstrosities like the Omni, for instance. They wanted to
identify and preserve, from a design standpoint, what was unique and
valuable to Miami. Right away, they latched onto south Miami Beach's 1930s'
Art Deco hotels, apartment houses, and storefronts.

The Miami Design Preservation League grew rapidly. Its first goal was to
gain National Register of Historic Places status for the south Miami Beach Art
Deco district. In 1978, Andrew Capitman, Barbara's oldest son, bought the
aging Cardozo Hotel at 1300 Ocean Drive for $800,000, which he didn't have
a penny of. To finance it, he structured and sold limited partnerships—a very
risky venture, but he pulled it off. At the time, no bank would touch property
in south Miami Beach. (In 1992, Gloria Estefan and husband Emilio would
buy the Cardozo for $5 million.) Shortly after the Cardozo purchase,
Andrew bought and renovated four more hotels. This broke the ice for the
revitalization of the district.

In 1979, the Miami Design Preservation League won designation for twenty

Marlin Hotel, Miami Beach

blocks—approximately one square mile—of south Miami Beach to be listed on the National Register of Historic Places. The area was officially referred to as the Miami Beach Architectural District. It was an unprecedented listing. This was the first designated historic district made up entirely of twentieth-century buildings. Most were Art Deco, some Spanish-Mediterranean. No single building stood out from the others. Instead, it was the sheer volume of buildings in one area—all built during a brief period and all reflecting one of two very distinct styles—that made this a unique place.

While the listing meant tax incentives for owners who would renovate the buildings, it did not guarantee that those buildings could not be torn down. That would require a local historic preservation ordinance, and Capitman wasted no time getting to work on it. This proved to be a much more daunting task than getting the national listing. Miami's city counsel, siding with condo developers, adamantly opposed it. A classic restoration-versus-new-development head-butting war took place, in the newspapers and in the courtroom, between Capitman and high-rise developers like Abe Resnick. Eventually, some sections of the district were granted historic protection, but not before several buildings were demolished, notably the 1940 New Yorker, the 1925 Boulevard, and the 1939 Senator.

By the mid-1980s, south Miami Beach was beginning to respond to resuscitation. Leonard Horowitz came up with an idea to breathe Technicolor life back into the buildings. He designed elaborate color schemes in bright pastels that emphasized the decorative features of their facades. This may not have been historically correct—in the 1930s, they were mostly painted white with some green or beige trim— but it was quite successful. Now these buildings—in all thirty-three Baskin-Robbins flavors—looked good enough to eat. It opened a lot of eyes and drew worldwide attention to the district. Suddenly south Miami Beach (or just "South Beach" for short) was the place for outdoor fashion shoots. It was on the cover of every magazine in every grocery store stand. Oddly enough, it may have been the cheesy TV show Miami Vice that ultimately secured South Beach's popularity. The show began in 1984 and was shot regularly in Miami Beach. The bright Art Deco hotels on Ocean Drive featured prominently in its opening credits.

Barbara Capitman's tireless efforts ultimately saved South Beach, but things didn't turn out exactly as she had planned. She and fellow Miami Design Preservation League members originally envisioned a district with distinct boundaries and buffer zones, with grand entrances and promenades. Still, no one can deny the phenomenal success of the district. The crusade consumed Barbara's life, drained her personal finances, and ultimately sapped her health, but she lived for it! One of her last great battles was to try to save the Senator Hotel at 12th Street and Collins Avenue. She succeeded in putting off its demolition for almost two years. Towards the end, she organized all-night, candlelit vigils on the Senator's front porch. At one point, she even chained herself to one the columns. In late 1988, it was torn down and replaced with a parking garage. A year and a half later, one week before her seventieth birthday, Barbara Capitman passed away.

Early Miami Beach History

OVER ITS ONE-HUNDRED-year history, Miami Beach has seesawed from mangrove swamp to tropical paradise, from land development boondoggle to retirement community, and from crime-ridden war zone to historically preserved architectural wonderland, international travel destination, and one of the hottest pieces of real estate in the country.

Prior to the turn of the twentieth century, what would later become Miami Beach had very little beach at all. It was no more than a mosquito-infested mangrove key like dozens more that dotted the coast. Locals simply referred to it as the Peninsula. Technically, it was a peninsula until 1924, when a storm washed away its thin sandbar connection to the mainland. The first to attempt to tame it was New Jerseyan John Lum. He arrived in 1882 and tried for three years to cultivate a coconut palm grove before giving up. Next came fellow New Jerseyan and Quaker farmer John Collins, who had originally loaned Lum money for the coconut palm grove. In 1909, the seventy-one-year-old Collins came to the Peninsula and successfully planted bananas, avocados, mangos, and any other tropical fruits or vegetables that he could make grow.

In 1910, millionaire, flamboyant promoter, inventor, and auto industry magnate Carl Fisher bought a vacation house across the bay from the Peninsula (a year after he began building the Indianapolis Motor Speedway). Two years later, Fisher happened across John Collins, who had by then begun the construction of a bridge to cross the bay from the Peninsula. Fisher financed the completion of the bridge in exchange for some of Collins' property. Next, Fisher acquired more property at the Peninsula's southern tip from brothers J. E. and J. N. Lummus, who were selling lots on what they were calling Ocean Beach. Fisher had the grand idea to build a resort city.

Fisher originally estimated that he could cut down the mangroves and dredge sand from the bottom of the bay to build the city's foundation for less than $100,000. He had drastically underestimated. It cost him that much for just two days of dredging. To the bewilderment of friends and business associates, Fisher plowed forward nonetheless, clearing the land and laying out the city. No doubt, he poured millions of dollars into the project that, in 1915, incorporated as Miami Beach. Fisher had built a golf course, a yacht basin, and the Lincoln Hotel, but it wasn't catching on. He even tried offering free lots to those who would build on them. World War I further stalled the town's development, but following its end in 1919, Fisher decided to add a polo field and horse stables to try to attract the wealthy elite. This may have marked the turning point in what most people, until then, had considered Fisher's colossal failure.

Art Deco and Tropical Art Deco

DESPITE THE GREAT DEPRESSION, south Miami Beach saw an explosion of development in the 1930s. During that decade, over 2,000 homes, 480 apartment houses, and 160 hotels were built there. Most went up between 1934 and 1941. Among a handful of astoundingly prolific architect/developers, three standouts—L. Murray Dixon, Henry Hohauser, and Albert Anis—were responsible for the lion's share of these buildings. Dixon came to Miami Beach in 1928 from New York, where he had worked at the firm of Schultze and Weaver, designers of the Waldorf-Astoria Hotel in New York and the just-completed Biltmore Hotel in Coral Gables (Miami). Hohauser, also from New York, had worked in a firm with his cousin William Hohauser. While he was second to Dixon in quantity, Hohauser's designs are considered more stylistic and elegant. Anis came from Chicago. All three were strongly influenced by the modern skyscrapers that were going up in their respective hometowns.

Art Deco was born of turn-of-the-century Paris fashion styles, with some Italian and German influence thrown in. A 1925 exhibit of design, architecture, and applied arts in Paris called the Exposition Internationale des Arts Decoratifs et Industriels Moderns (Art Deco for short, although that term was not coined until the 1960s) showed the Moderne style to the world. Its intention was to shift design influences away from the "old" Classic, Victorian, and Revival styles. Twenty countries exhibited their finest modern designs. Although invited, the United States did not officially participate, but some Americans did attend. One was Cedric Gibbons, then the supervising art director at MGM Studios. He returned to the States so impressed with what he had seen that he copied the style for many of MGM's movie sets. This was one of the ways that Art Deco gained wide exposure in the United States. In 1928, Gibbons designed one of the most recognizable Art Deco figures: the Academy Awards' Oscar.

The new style reflected a societal desire to emerge from the Depression and to move ahead. Art Deco looked to a future of technological advances. Its arrival coincided with the big band/swing era and with the birth of commercial aviation. It was considered futuristic, fanciful, and optimistic. Two famous examples are the 1930 Chrysler Building and the 1931 Empire State Building, both in New York. And it wasn't just for skyscrapers—gas stations and movie houses were popular "Moderne" subjects.

The Moderne design trend influenced not only architecture but also automobiles, trains, ships, furniture, even toasters and salt-and-pepper shakers. The style can be divided into a variety of substyles, among them Zigzig Moderne, which tends to be more ornamented and decorative;

Depression Moderne, more stark and simplistic (a style used frequently in the late 1930s and early 1940s for government buildings); and Streamline Moderne, my favorite. Streamline borrowed heavily from aerodynamics—wind sculpted, with all sharp angles rounded off. These buildings looked like they were going ninety miles per hour! They mimicked the sleek new trains, ocean liners, and airplanes. This was the Flash Gordon style.

Miami Beach Art Deco mixed in its own tropical flavor: bas-relief sculptures and scenes etched in glass depicted pelicans, herons, flamingos, flowers, and palm trees. Builders frequently used local coral block for window framing and archways. A nautical influence was common—porthole windows; wrap-around, protruding "eyebrow" shades; stainless steel trim; ship railings; and decorative friezes with dolphins or waves. Architects paid homage to their favorite skyscrapers with soaring pylons or needlelike finials above entry-ways and with stepped-back, segmented facades that gave the buildings a multidimensional look. These guys were one-man shows, choosing and designing every detail themselves, right down to the light fixtures. The tropi-cal deco style continued into the interiors. Terrazzo floors—often tinted in various colors and poured in geometric patterns to match the decor—were common. Glass block was strategically placed to let light (but not heat) into lobbies. Recessed and indirect lighting was popular. Often, architects would hire local artists to paint elaborate murals if the budget allowed.

Miami Beach's building boom may have taken place despite the Great Depression, but it was not unaffected by it. Beneath their stylized facades, these were simple two-, three-, and occasionally four-story, inexpensive-to-build, stucco-on-block structures. While the designers knew these buildings had to be cheap to build, they were not about to let their creations be boring. Working within the constraints of Depression-era economics, they were deter-mined to put up buildings—especially hotels—that had pizzazz and that conveyed a sense of optimism about the future.

Since a Miami Beach city ordinance declared the official start of the tourist season as December 16, there was always a feverish rush to complete con-struction by the deadline. All work had to stop by midnight on December 15 so that tourists could enjoy their visits in tranquillity.

The biggest year of construction was 1941. Forty-one hotels and one hundred sixty apartment buildings went up. It was also the last year. Pearl Harbor brought the boom to a grinding halt. Military branches hastily con-verted most of the hotels into barracks for troops who trained on the beach.

South Miami Beach Hotel Choices

THE OCEAN DRIVE (THAT'S the beach road) hotels tend to be louder, rowdier, more in the middle of all the action. The Collins Avenue hotels (one block inland from Ocean Drive) are equally refined as—and in some cases more so than—those on Ocean Drive. They are generally more quiet and more subdued, except for the Marlin—that's a wild place! Take your pick.

Auto traffic crawls in South Beach, and parking is difficult at best, but the community likes it that way. South Beach always was, and still is, intended to be a walking community. South Beach's hotel-front outdoor cafés remind me of what I might expect to see in Paris or Monaco. This is in contrast to the north section of Miami Beach and its giant hotels popularized by Jackie Gleason in the 1960s. Of course, the night life on South Beach is crazy—and Sunday night, particularly after midnight, is the big night. By the way, if you're thinking about bringing kids here to go to the beach, be forewarned—they are liable to see more (as in, less bathing suit) than they are accustomed to. Frankly, this isn't a great place to bring kids.

Avalon and Majestic

700 Ocean Drive
660 Ocean Drive
Miami Beach, Florida 33139
(800) 933-3306
(305) 538-0133
vacation@southbeach
hotels.com/sbh.htm
www.southbeachhotels.com

106 rooms, $89–220
Continental breakfast

LOOK FOR THEIR SIGNATURE 1950s-vintage Chevy convertible parked out front. This is actually two hotels operated as one. The Avalon, built in 1940, was designed by Albert Anis.

Avalon and
Majestic

Blue Moon Hotel

Blue Moon Hotel
944 Collins Avenue
Miami Beach, Florida 33139
(800) 724-1623
(305) 673-2262
bluemoon@merv.com
www.merv.com/blue_moon

75 rooms, $69–295

ORIGINALLY CALLED THE LAFAYETTE, the Blue Moon was designed by Henry J. Maloney and built in 1934. The architecture leans more toward Italian than Art Deco. It was completely restored in 1993. During the restoration, the beautiful original tile floors in the lobby were retained. Merv Griffin bought the hotel in 1998 and renamed it the Blue Moon.

Beacon Hotel
720 Ocean Drive
Miami Beach, Florida 33139
(800) 649-7075
(305) 674-8200
(305) 674-8976 fax
reservations@beacon-hotel.com
www.beacon-hotel.com

80 rooms, $105–335

THIS IS A 1936-1937 Henry O. Nelson design, remodeled in 1998. It sits right in the middle of Ocean Drive action.

Beacon Hotel

Cavalier Hotel

Cavalier Hotel
1320 Ocean Drive
Miami Beach, Florida 33139
(800) 688-7678
(305) 531-8800
(305) 604-5000
(305) 531-5543 fax
reservations@islandoutpost.com
www.islandoutpost.com/Cavalier

42 rooms and 3 suites, $130–375

A ROY F. FRANCE design, the Cavalier was built in 1936. Chris Blackwell, founder of Island Records (the late Bob Marley's label), bought and restored six hotels, including the Cavalier, on south Miami Beach in the mid-1990s. He also owns and operates properties in Jamaica and the Bahamas.

Casa Grande Hotel
834 Ocean Drive
Miami Beach, Florida 33139
(800) 688-7678
(305) 672-7003
(305) 531-8800
reservations@islandoutpost.com
www.islandoutpost.com/CasaGrande

34 rooms and suites, $195-1500

ANOTHER CHRIS BLACKWELL HOTEL, this one is very plush and expensive. The interior is beautifully decorated in an Asian-Indonesian style. Most of the rooms are suites with kitchens.

Cardozo Hotel
1300 Ocean Drive
Miami Beach, Florida 33139
(800) 782-6500
(305) 535-6500
www.cardozohotel.com

44 rooms, $150–620

Cardozo Hotel

THE CARDOZO WAS ANDREW Capitman's first project, bought and restored in 1978–1979. Gloria Estefan and husband Emilio bought and re-refurbished it in 1992. Its rounded corners and prominent eyebrows are classic Streamline Deco. Designed by Henry Hohauser and built in 1939, the Cardozo was named after Supreme Court Justice Benjamin Cardozo. The 1959 Frank Sinatra movie *A Hole in the Head* was filmed here.

Colony Hotel

736 Ocean Drive
Miami Beach, Florida 33139
(800) 226-5669
(305) 673-0088
(305) 532-0762 fax
www.colonyhotel-sobe.com

50 rooms, $99–220
full breakfast

BUILT IN 1939, THE Colony is another Henry Hohauser design and is probably the most-photographed South Beach hotel. It's right in the middle of Ocean Drive. You can't miss its famous, vertical, blue neon sign at night.

Colony Hotel

Essex House
1001 Collins Avenue
Miami Beach, Florida 33139
(800) 553-7739
(305) 534-2700
(305) 532-3827 fax
info@essexhotel.com
www.essexhotel.com

61 rooms and 19 suites, $109–369

THIS IS A TERRIFIC example of Nautical Deco, with octagonal porthole windows and a corner entryway that reminds me of a ship's prow. It was designed by Henry Hohauser and built in 1938. One must-see is the beautiful Earl LaPan Everglades mural above the lobby fireplace. LaPan painted it in 1938, then returned to do its restoration in 1989.

Impala Hotel
1228 Collins Avenue
Miami Beach, Florida 33139
(800) 646-7252
(305) 673-2021
(305) 673-5984 fax
impala@travelbase.com
www.hotelimpalamiamibeach.com

17 rooms and suites, $175–400

CURRENT OWNERS ANGELA RANDALL and Janice Vallery purchased the Impala in 1998. It had gone through an extensive renovation in 1994. Although it was built during the Art Deco explosion in the 1930s, this is not an Art Deco building. The architecture is more Italian-Mediterranean. The Impala is one of my favorites because it is so calm, a sanctuary in the middle of all the craziness of South Beach. It reminds me of the small "boutique" hotels usually found only in Europe. The well-shaded side courtyard will teleport you to Paris or Monte Carlo. The interior is elegant, yet still inviting and comfortable. The Italian tile floor adds to the European style. The tile was originally slated to go onto the floor of Gianni Versace's mansion—his loss was the Impala's gain.

Angela showed me the posh Grand Suite, number 210. It is the front center room on the second floor with its own private balcony. This is an elegant hotel with old-world ambiance

Impala Hotel

Kent Hotel

1311 Collins Avenue
Miami Beach, Florida 33139
(800) 688-7678
(305) 604-5000
(305) 531-8800
reservations@islandoutpost.com
www.islandoutpost.com/Kent

52 rooms and suites, $100–275

ANOTHER CHRIS BLACKWELL RESTORATION, the Kent was designed by L. Murray Dixon and built in 1939. This is one of the more reasonably priced of the Art Deco hotels in South Beach. Look for the space needle.

Leslie Hotel
1244 Ocean Drive
Miami Beach, Florida 33139
(800) 688-7678
(305) 604-5000
(305) 531-8800
reservations@islandoutpost.com
www.islandoutpost.com/Leslie

39 rooms and 4 suites, $130–375

PUT ON YOUR SUNGLASSES—not just so you'll look cool, but because you'll need them just to look at the bright yellow Leslie Hotel. The loud tropical colors continue into the interior. Another Chris Blackwell property, the Leslie was designed by Albert Anis and built in 1937.

Leslie Hotel

Hotel Ocean

1230 Ocean Drive
Miami Beach, Florida 33139
(800) 783-1725
(305) 672-2579
(305) 672-7665 fax
info@hotelocean.com
www.hotelocean.com

27 rooms and suites, $169–515
Continental breakfast, pets accepted

THIS IS A LUXURIOUS, European-style hotel that actually allows you to bring your pets.

The Tides

1220 Ocean Drive
Miami Beach, Florida 33139
(800) 688-7678
(305) 531-8800
reservations@islandoutpost.com
www.islandoutpost.com/Tides

45 rooms and suites, $350–2,000

The Tides

CHRIS BLACKWELL STRIKES AGAIN. The Tides is a nine-story-tall, 1936 L. Murray Dixon hotel. This one is very upscale, with expansive (and expensive) rooms and suites.

Marlin Hotel
1200 Collins Avenue
Miami Beach, Florida 33139
(800) 688-7678
(305) 531-8800
reservations@islandoutpost.com
www.islandoutpost.com/Marlin

12 suites, $195–325

CHRIS BLACKWELL DID A wild renovation in 1994 on this 1939 L. Murray Dixon hotel. Chris's South Beach Studios recording studio is here. The lobby is done up in stainless steel, and the lobby lounge is right out of the psychedelic sixties. It's a popular hangout and after-midnight hot spot.

Marlin Hotel

Pelican Hotel
826 Ocean Drive
Miami Beach, Florida 33139
(305) 673-3373
(800) 773-5422
(305) 673-3255 fax
pelican@pelicanhotel.com
www.pelicanhotel.com

30 rooms and suites, $135–400

THIS IS A POST-deco (early 1950s) hotel, pretty low-key on the outside but absolutely bizarre on the inside! It was renovated by the Diesel Jeans Company in 1994; each room was eclectically decorated in a different theme by designer Magnus Ehrland. The Me Tarzan, You Vain room is one of the wildest. With African statues and (presumably faux) zebra skins, it resembles a room in a Tanzanian lodge. Others include Up, Up in the Sky, with airplane parts and jet fighter models; Best Whorehouse, done up in bordello extraordinaire; and 1970s-style Psychedelicate Girl. Then there's People from the Sixties, Bang a Boomerang, and High Corral, OK Chaparral. You get the idea. The cat's meow is the penthouse suite, called simply The Penthouse Suite, with its own private rooftop deck and hot tub. Inside it has a full kitchen that would please any restaurant chef, a dining room with eight-place dining table, a video wall with nine screens, and a giant fish tank built into the living room wall. Oh, yes— and there are three bedrooms and two baths.

Miami Design Preservation League/Art Deco Center
1001 Ocean Drive
Miami Beach, Florida 33139
(305) 672-2014
(305) 531-3484

THE MIAMI DESIGN PRESERVATION League puts on the Art Deco Weekend festival on the third weekend in January. The Art Deco Center conducts tours.

Wolfie's Delicatessen
2038 Collins Avenue
Miami Beach, Florida 33139
(305) 538-6626

WOLFIE'S IS WHERE, IN the 1950s and 1960s, organized crime figure Meyer Lansky ate lunch almost every day. Lansky was considered to have been the brains behind the Mob, the guy who actually organized organized crime. Unlike his flashy gangster counterparts, Lansky dressed and conducted himself—at least outwardly—as any other retiree on Miami Beach. I've read that Wolfie's chocolate cake was his favorite.

Joe's Stone Crab
227 Biscayne Street
Miami Beach, Florida 33139
(305) 673-0365

THE ORIGINAL STONE CRAB restaurant. OK, so it's a tourist spot. (Hey, this is Miami Beach.) And they don't take reservations. And a two-hour wait is not unusual. But stone crab is the food of the gods!

Coral Gables

Another Amazing Miami Real Estate Boom Story

HISTORIANS DESCRIBE GEORGE EDGAR Merrick variously as a dreamer, a poet, a schemer, a philanthropist, a visionary, a darn good salesman, an extraordinary success, and a crushing failure. He was all of these things. George was twelve when his father, Reverend Soloman Merrick, moved the family from Massachusetts to Florida. It was 1898, and Reverend Merrick had chosen a farm a few miles south of the land that Mrs. Tuttle had split with Henry Flagler two years prior. The Merricks did well in citrus farming. Soloman Merrick built the family a large house from locally mined oolitic limestone, which he mistakenly referred to as coral when he named their home Coral Gables. When his father died in 1911, George inherited the farm.

George Merrick wasn't all that excited about farming. His vision was to design and build the perfect planned city. He began acquiring land around the family homestead. With the help of his uncle Denman Fink, architect Phineas Paist, and landscape architect Frank Button, the grand community of Coral Gables came to life—on paper. While he had garnered some financial backing, Merrick needed to pre-sell many lots to finance the whole venture. Fortunately, Merrick knew how to promote. The lots sold almost as fast as they went up for sale. Many sold sight-unseen. Through a combination of good timing and clever marketing, Merrick's plan was a success and he built the city of his dreams. It had (and still has) beautiful parks, tree-lined boulevards, its own university (the University of Miami, which opened in 1926), and something quite novel for its time—very strict building codes and architectural restrictions.

The Biltmore Hotel
1200 Anastasia Avenue
Coral Gables, Florida 33134
(800) 727-1926
(305) 445-8066
(305) 913-3159 fax
www.biltmorehotel.com

245 rooms and 35 suites, $239–2,650
pool, tennis courts, golf course, fitness center, restaurant

THE LAST GREAT ADDITION to Merrick's Coral Gables was the majestic Miami Biltmore Hotel. Begun in 1924 and completed in 1926, the fifteen-story (including its tower) hotel was the result of a partnership with Biltmore Hotels chain owner John McEntee Bowman. The grandeur was short-lived. In September 1926, a devastating hurricane struck Miami head-on. The new town was pummeled by 130-mile-per-hour winds. Three years later, the stock market crash finished the job that the hurricane had started. Merrick was completely wiped out.

George Merrick left Coral Gables and drifted down to the Upper Keys, where he ran a fishing camp—until it was demolished by the 1935 Labor Day hurricane, the most powerful ever to strike North America. Merrick returned to Miami and at first dabbled in real estate again. Then, from 1940 until his death in 1942 at age fifty-six, he was postmaster of Miami.

Sometimes a person's life must be viewed many years in retrospect to judge whether he was a success or a failure. George Merrick's dreams did come true, although some came years after he was gone. Coral Gables turned into the beautiful community he had envisioned. No doubt, the University of Miami far exceeded his expectations. Perhaps some of the most important things he left behind were his city planning ideas and design philosophy, still considered the textbook model for developers today. Lastly, there is the Biltmore Hotel. Although it cycled through some very rough times and was almost slated for demolition in the 1970s, today the Biltmore is everything Merrick wanted it to be and more.

The Miami Biltmore was a $10-million project when construction began

The Biltmore Hotel

(remember, that's in 1920s' dollars). Trainloads of guests came from up and down the eastern seaboard to attend its 1926 grand opening. The Biltmore positioned itself as host to the elite—British royalty, Hollywood movie stars, politicians, and wealthy industrialists—but it was up against tough times. The 1926 hurricane had wreaked havoc on the surrounding community. The stock market crash of 1929 kept potential travelers at home. Then in 1931, following John McEntee Bowman's death, the Biltmore Hotel chain filed for bankruptcy.

Despite these circumstances, the Miami Biltmore managed to remain open through the 1930s. In an attempt to attract what clientele they could during the depressed times, its owners hosted swimming exhibition events in their giant, twenty-one-thousand-square-foot swimming pool. A young Johnny Weissmuller was swimming coach there for a while and actually broke a world swimming record in the Biltmore pool.

During World War II, the hotel was converted into an Army Air Forces regional hospital. After that, it was a Veterans Administration hospital until 1968, when it closed its doors. The Biltmore remained boarded-up through the 1970s. The city of Coral Gables had gained ownership through the Historic Monuments Act and Legacy of Parks Program, but nothing was done with it until 1983, when the city began to refurbish it. It took four years and over $50 million to complete the major restoration. On New Year's Eve in 1987, the Biltmore reopened. Three years later, it closed again. Seaway Hotels bought it in 1992 and re-reopened it after even more restoration. This time it seems to have worked!

Among other improvements, Seaway added a health club and spa. Today's Biltmore is just what George Merrick hoped it would be. It is a grand and luxurious hotel, done in Spanish-Mediterranean architecture with a Spanish barrel-tile roof and a center tower patterned after the Giraldo Tower in Seville, Spain. It has a lush, gardenlike courtyard with a central fountain, all overlooking the Coral Gables Golf Course. The ornate main ballroom, with its towering stone columns, is more than suitable for entertaining royalty.

The Biltmore has had its share of famous guests throughout its on-again-off-again lifetime: Bing Crosby, Judy Garland, Douglas Fairbanks, Lauren Bacall, Robert Redford, Barbara Bush, even royalty—the Duke and Duchess of Windsor. The most infamous guest was Al Capone, who stayed in the tower suite (now called the Everglades Suite but better known as the Capone Suite) while hiding out from law enforcement officials.

The Everglades Suite occupies the thirteenth and fourteenth floors. Everglades scenes are painted on its domed ceiling. It has its own kitchen, Jacuzzi, and stone fireplace. The hotel can even arrange for butler service if that's what you are accustomed to. The Merrick Suite is the entire fifteenth floor beneath the tower. It has three bedrooms and baths, a fireplace, and two balconies to take in the best view at the hotel. The Biltmore's La Palme d'Or Restaurant regularly brings in guest chefs from famous restaurants in France.

Hotel Place St. Michel

162 Alcazar Avenue
Coral Gables, Florida 33134
(305) 444-1666
(800) 848-4683

27 rooms, $125–200
Continental breakfast, gourmet restaurant

THIS THREE-STORY SPANISH architecture hotel was designed by Addison Mizner, who created the city of Boca Raton. It opened as the Hotel Sevilla in 1926, the same year as the Biltmore. Today, it is known as much for its excellent restaurant as for its accommodations.

Tavernier

THE HURRICANE OF 1935

MOST PEOPLE ASSUME THAT Hurricane Andrew was the most powerful storm to hit the United States in the twentieth century. As devastating as it was, another surpassed it in strength.

On September 1, 1935, locals on the Lower and Upper (Islamorada) Matecumbe Keys were boarding up their homes in preparation for a tropical storm that was crossing the Bahamas. Weather forecasters were predicting that it would pass south of Key West. By the morning of September 2, Labor Day, barometers on the Matecumbe Keys were dropping rapidly. That meant that the storm had veered to the northeast and was gaining strength.

The offspring of three pioneer Keys families populated Upper Matecumbe. The Russells, the Pinders, and the Parkers had sailed here in the mid- and late 1800s from the Bahamas. These Anglo-Bahamian settlers were called "Conchs" after the shellfish that was such a staple in their diet. They built their homes from driftwood, planted pineapple and key lime groves, and fished. In 1905, their island outpost became connected with the rest of civilization when Henry Flagler built his railroad through here on its way to Key West. Several hotels and vacation homes went up on Islamorada. Another hotel went up in Tavernier. Flagler built a fishing camp on Long Key.

In the fall of 1935, the Veterans Administration sent 680 unemployed World War I veterans to the Upper Keys to build roads and bridges. The press referred to them as "bonus-marching veterans" because they had marched on

Washington, D. C., to protest that they could not get jobs after returning from the war and that they wanted their war bonuses accelerated. The road work veterans were living in three construction camps on Upper and Lower Matecumbe Keys. About two thirds of them had gone to Miami or Key West for the Labor Day holiday. Those who remained met a horrible fate.

By nightfall, the winds were howling, and it was apparent that this would be a "big one." Families huddled in their wood-frame "conch" bungalows and storm shelters. At 8:30 P.M., the barometer read an all-time record low pressure for the Northern hemisphere of 26.35 millibars.

The hurricane cut a swath right through Upper Matecumbe. Winds blew to 260 miles per hour. A twenty-foot tidal wave swept the islands, ripping whole houses with families in them off their foundations. Roger Albury and his nine family members were in their eight-room Tavernier house when the wave picked it up and carried it over two hundred feet.

Earlier in the day, an eleven-car passenger train had left Miami to try to evacuate the Upper Keys residents and the war veteran road workers. It reached Islamorada right when the wall of water struck, blasting each of the one-hundred-ton passenger cars right off its tracks. Only the loco-motive remained upright. It was the last train to travel these tracks. Flagler's company never rebuilt the railroad.

Seventeen-year-old Bernard Russell and his family sought shelter in his father's Islamorada lime-packing house. When floodwaters came pouring in, they tried to escape to higher ground. Clinging desperately to each other, they pushed out of the packing house and were instantly blown apart from one another. Bernard's sister and his young nephew were torn from his hands. Of the sixty members of the extended Russell family, only eleven survived the hurricane.

Ultimately, 408 bodies were counted, but the actual death toll was probably twice that. The hurricane killed all of the war veteran road workers who had stayed on the islands. Months after the storm, remains of victims' bodies were still being recovered. Thirty years later, while dredging on an outlying key near Islamorada, a developer found an automobile with 1935 license plates and five skeletons inside.

Ernest Hemingway wrote a scathing newspaper editorial on September 17, 1935 entitled "Who Murdered the Vets?". Hemingway was living in Key West at the time of the hurricane and had gone to the Upper Keys with crews to assist in the rescue efforts two days after the disaster. His article was an angry indictment of the newly formed Veterans Administration for sending the veter-ans down to the Keys to work during the most dangerous part of the hurricane season. It reads in part, ". . . fishermen such as President Herbert Hoover, and

President Roosevelt, do not come to the Florida Keys in hurricane months. . . . There is a known danger to property. . . . But veterans, especially the bonus-marching variety, are not property. They are only human beings; unsuccessful human beings, and all they have to lose are their lives. They are doing coolie labor, for a top wage of $45 a month, and they have been put down on the Florida Keys where they can't make trouble."

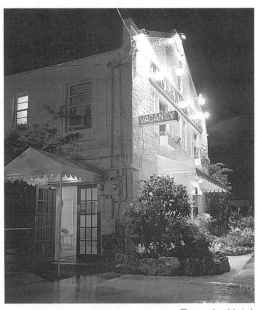

Tavernier Hotel

The long and painful process of rebuilding began immediately after the storm had passed and the bodies were buried. The young Bernard Russell, who had seen his family all but wiped out, remained on the island to take part in the rebuilding. He started his own cabinet-building/carpentry business and later founded Islamorada's first fire rescue department. He still lives on Islamorada, just a few blocks from the Hurricane Memorial. In a 1991 *St. Petersburg Times* interview, he said, "The thing I have always asked myself is this: Why was I spared? Why am I still here? I saw great big robust he-men, dead on the ground. I saw little skinny children who survived. How do you put that together in your mind? I have to think the Lord might have a purpose for me. I might be needed."

Tavernier Hotel

91865 Overseas Highway (Highway 1)
Mile marker 91.8
Tavernier, Florida 33070
(305) 852-4131
(800) 515-4131
(305) 852-4037 fax
TavHotel@aol.com
www.tavernierhotel.com

17 rooms, $59–119
restaurant, fitness room, hot tub, refrigerators in all rooms

THE PINK AND PEACH, concrete-block Tavernier Hotel and Copper Kettle Restaurant is one of the few Tavernier structures that predates the hurricane of 1935. The current hotel is actually several buildings. In 1928, Mac McKenzie built and operated a small drugstore and gas station here. The drugstore building now houses the Copper Kettle, and the old gas station has been converted into one of the Tavernier Hotel's suites.

McKenzie began construction on a theater adjacent to the drugstore and the gas station in 1934. He was almost ready for its grand opening when the 1935 hurricane struck. The two-story theater, like his other structures, was sturdy. Built from concrete, it managed to withstand the onslaught. When the Red Cross arrived following the devastation, they needed housing for the survivors and temporary medical facilities. McKenzie's theater building was better than they could have wished for.

A year later, the Red Cross' work was done, and Mac McKenzie finally opened his theater. However, the storm left the area's economy and population decimated, and there was little interest in going to a theater. After operating it for a year, he closed the doors. Down but not out, and not wanting to waste a perfectly good building, Mac remodeled the interior and converted it into a hotel/boarding house called the Tavernier Hotel.

Today's Tavernier Hotel caters to vacationing travelers, many of them scuba divers and sport fishermen. The Keys sit on top of the only living coral reef in the continental United States and offer some of the best fishing and scuba diving in the world. The hotel's Copper Kettle Restaurant has indoor and outdoor dining with an English tearoom atmosphere. Try the Fish and Grits for breakfast (I did—trust me, it's delicious) or the traditional English Fish and Chips for dinner.

Big Pine Key

BIG PINE KEY, THE largest island in the Lower Keys, and its neighbor, No Name Key, are home to a number of rare and endangered birds, reptiles, and mammals, including the short-eared Lower Keys marsh rabbit and the petite Key deer.

In 1957, the U. S. Fish and Wildlife Service established the National Key Deer Refuge on Big Pine Key and No Name Key. Hunters had all but decimated the Key deer population. They numbered fewer than fifty in 1949. The refuge's first manager, Jack Watson, fought vehemently for their survival and is credited with saving them, almost singlehandedly, from extinction.

Publicizing the National Key Deer Refuge is a double-edged sword:

the potential for more traffic on the islands must be weighed against the value of an increased awareness of the Key deer's plight. Every person I spoke to in the community said something to me about driving slowly and carefully (whether I asked about it or not). The local police do their part. They write speeding tickets for just one mile per hour over the limit, which is thirty-five miles per hour most everywhere on the island.

The Barnacle Bed and Breakfast

1557 Long Beach Road
Big Pine Key, Florida 33043
(305) 872-3298
(800) 465-9100
http://cust.iamerica.net/barnacle

4 rooms, $85–125
full breakfast, kayaks, scuba diving trips

BIG PINE KEY IS DECIDEDLY quieter and more leisurely than its famous neighbor thirty-five miles to the south. That's what I was looking for when I found the Barnacle Bed & Breakfast, a place where leisure has been elevated to an art form.

Long Beach Road looks a little like it is being reclaimed by the native flora. It dead-ends a short way past the Barnacle, so there is no traffic on it. A simple limestone wall marks the Barnacle's entrance. This place is an architectural enigma. Its style doesn't fall neatly into any conventional category. Modern? Eclectic? Nautical? Tropical? There are no right angles. Its pipe railings, archways, and generous open-air balcony remind me more than anything else of an ocean liner, albeit with an exterior painted in varying shades of earth tones reminiscent of the 1970s. From the top-floor, sunrise-watching deck (the ocean liner's bow), guests can scan the Atlantic's vivid turquoise water for rolling dolphin or maybe a jumping manta ray.

My room, the downstairs "ocean room," (done in shades of pastel sea green and plum), opens directly onto the beach. Multicolored, hexagonal tiles cover the floor. Creative use of space for the bathroom, kitchenette, and shelving reminds me of a state room on the Queen Elizabeth. Again, the walls are skewed at odd angles, the floor plan a series of triangles. My bed sits in its own little alcove that faces the ocean through sliding glass doors.

Original owner Steven "Woody" Cornell designed and built the Barnacle in 1976. Dive operators Tim and Jane Marquis bought it from Woody in 1994. "We didn't see any reason to change much of anything that Woody had built," Jane explains in her casual Louisiana accent. "I don't know how Woody came

The Barnacle

up with the design for this place, but it is definitely an original. Tim and I had been coming down here for years before we bought this place. We love it—it's quiet, laid-back, not rush-rush. We've been in the scuba diving trip business for over twenty years, and buying the Barnacle turned out to be the perfect complement. We can combine a stay here with customized dive packages—out to Looe Key or wherever the customer wants to go—or with fishing trips. We also own five boats. Business is mostly through word-of-mouth, and lately through our Internet web site."

If the house is an ocean liner, then the beach is the tropical port of call. Five steps outside my room, coconut palms with hammocks strung between them line the shore. More hammocks swing in the breeze under a thatched-roof hut. Tim and Jane offer all kinds of exploration amenities for their guests: kayaks, canoes, sailboats. They also organize fishing and diving trips—I chose an early afternoon nap in a hammock.

Jane serves a full breakfast in the Barnacle's alfresco second-floor central area (I'll call it the lobby, for lack of a better label). We feasted on blueberry pancakes, sausage, fresh-cut fruit, and fresh orange juice while enjoying the feel and smell of the salt breeze. I crawled back into that hammock before noon.

Little Torch Key

Little Palm Island
Mile Marker 28.5 (offices)
28500 Overseas Highway
Little Torch Key, Florida 33042
(305) 872-2524
(800) 343-8567
(305) 872-4843 fax
(305) 872-2551 (dinner-only reservations)
getlost@littlepalmisland.com
www.littlepalmisland.com

30 villas, $550–1,600
private island with ferry from Little Torch Key, seaplane transport directly to and from island available, gourmet restaurant, two meal plans ($125–140 per person per day or à la carte), health spa and fitness facility, PADI-certified scuba diving shop and two dive boats, dive trips, scuba certification courses, seaplane trips, sailing and fishing charters (various fees), kayaks, canoes, Windsurfers, small sailboats, beach, life-size chessboard, pool, rods and reels, masks and snorkels (included with stay), children over 16 welcome, non-smoking

WHAT IF ROBINSON CRUSOE'S island had had air conditioning, a gourmet restaurant with a five-star chef, a health spa, a scuba diving shop and boat, and, oh yeah, its own seaplane, and you could share it all with a handful of friends? Little Palm Island Resort and Spa, three miles out in the Atlantic Ocean off Little Torch Key, is just such a place. It's what Thurston Howell III would really have preferred.

It used to be called Sheriff's Island when John Spottswood owned it. He was sheriff of Monroe County and later Florida state senator. Harry Truman and his wife were regular guests back then. It evolved into a private fishing camp for statesmen and other VIPs. In addition to the Trumans, the Roosevelts, Kennedys, and Nixons were all guests at one time or another.

Restaurateur Ben Woodson, along with a group of investors, purchased the island in 1986 and built the Little Palm Island Resort, which opened in 1988. It has recently been acquired by the Noble House Hotel and Resorts Group out of Kirkland, Washington, which also owns, among others, the Ocean Key Resort in Key West, the Grove Island Club and Resort in Coconut Grove, and the Portofino Hotel and Yacht Club in Redondo Beach, California. Heinrich Morio is now the resort's manager.

Little Palm Island's own *Little Palm Air* Cessna 206 floatplane, which accommodates four passengers with thirty pounds of luggage each, will pick you up at Miami International or Ft. Lauderdale International Airport and deliver you directly to the island's private beach (for an added fee). It will also take you on excursions to the Dry Tortugas, the Everglades, or most anywhere in the Keys—just ask. Most guests arrive by ferry from Little Torch Key (next to Big Pine Key), and some come in their own boats. Dockage is available for guests.

This lima bean-shaped, five-acre island has fourteen bungalows, each of which contains two one-bedroom suites. In addition, there are two new Island Grand suites, which are larger than the bungalows and have their own hot tubs and his-and-her bathrooms. All of the bungalows and Island Grand suites have genuine palm-thatched roofs, indoor/outdoor showers, and private decks. From the outside, they appear island-rustic, like huts on Fiji or Palau. Inside they are elegant and luxurious, if not Hemingwayesque—king-size four-poster beds with mosquito-net canopies (for ambiance only, the hosts are quick to point out!), British Colonial furniture, and, of course, air conditioning. There are, however, no phones, televisions, or alarm clocks in the rooms. If you insist on checking in with the office, Harry Truman's old outhouse has been converted into a phone booth.

The Great House, the renovated original 1938 pecky cypress fishing lodge, houses the multiple-award-winning restaurant. Chef Adam Votaw prepares sumptuous, tropical-inspired dishes such as pan-seared yellow snapper with lobster dumplings in tamarind-pineapple juice with watermelon relish on the side. Top off your meal with exotic desserts like spiced honey café con leche cake.

Little Palm Island is perhaps a bit more South Pacific than Florida-Caribbean in appearance. A natural, white-sand beach—rare in the Keys and deposited by rapid currents in Newfound Harbor Channel—wraps around one end. Coconut palm trees lean out over the sand and the emerald waters. Hibiscus, oleander, and bougainvillea grow wild everywhere. Back in 1962, Warner Brothers filmed the movie *PT 109*, which was set in the South Pacific, here.

Less than five miles away is Looe Key National Marine Sanctuary, one of the most beautiful underwater spots in the Keys. The Little Palm Island dive shop operates two thirty-foot boats for diving at Looe Key and also on the *Adolphus Busch,* a recently sunk freighter. Day and moonlight sailing charters on a forty-two-foot yacht, deep-sea and flats fishing, seaplane excursions, and a full-service spa and fitness facility mean there's never a reason to leave the island.

Little Palm Island Resort is not an inexpensive place, but it is considered by many travel experts to be Florida's ultimate getaway. Who knows? While you're there, you might run into Ginger and Mary Ann or the Professor.

Key West

WITH A FLAVOR MORE Caribbean than American, Key West revels in its irreverence and celebrates its eccentricity. Duval Street, the main street in Old Town Key West, parties until sunrise every night. The island's annual Fantasy Fest, which takes place the last week of October, makes Mardi Gras look like a debutante ball. In April 1982, Key West seceded from the United States and declared itself the independent Conch Republic in protest of a drug-search roadblock constructed by the government that halted all road traffic out of the Keys for about a week.

Some of this quirkiness can be attributed to Key West's remote location; it is the southernmost city in the continental United States. Mostly, though, I think it is the odd, the outcast, the outspoken, and the anything-but-conventional Key Westers who give the town its flavor. Native-born residents call themselves "Conchs." The term dates back to some of the Key's early pioneers who came from the Bahamas. In the 1780s, many British Loyalists who fled the United States following the American Revolution settled in the Abacos, the northernmost of the Bahamian out islands. In the mid-1800s, descendants of these Loyalists came to the Keys. Conch, a large shellfish plentiful in the waters off the Keys, was a staple in their diet, and the nickname stuck. Eventually the name evolved to include anyone born in the Keys.

The Abaco/British Loyalists were renowned boat builders and wood-working craftsmen. Key West "Conch architecture" owes much of its style to the skills of these people, many of whom found work here in construction. The typical Conch house blended Victorian style with Bahamian function and included steep tin roofs that collected rainwater into cisterns, deep (often two-story) wraparound porches, slat shutters that shaded large windows while still allowing the breeze to blow through, scuppers (roof hatches that vented hot air), and, of course, the intricate gingerbread trim favored by the more artistically inclined craftsmen. Occasionally, builders incorporated salvaged pieces from wrecked ships into the homes, such as porthole windows and brass railings (many of the furnishings were also salvage). Some houses were built with cupolas, or widow's walks, on their roofs, from which wreckers scanned the reefs and wives watched for returning seafaring husbands.

My favorite Key West pastime is to bicycle or moped through Old Town's residential back streets, where many of these houses still stand. Some, as you will see, have been restored as inns and bed & breakfasts. Tourism may be Key West's primary industry, and it can be a tacky, touristy place (particularly on Duval Street and around Mallory Square), but walk or ride a couple of blocks away from the mayhem and you will find rich, exciting history and quaint and often well-preserved architecture.

Key West is the westernmost of the Florida Keys, so the name seems appropriate from a geographical point of view. However, it is likely that the name Key West is really a mispronounced version of Cayo Hueso, Spanish for "Island of Bones." Spanish explorers and fishermen in the 1700s reported finding piles of bones on the island's shore. Most historians believe that these were the remains of a band of Calusa Indians who lost a terrible battle on Key West.

Historians are less certain who the victors in that battle were. Some think that the Tequesta Indians, who inhabited Florida's southeast coast, chased a faction of Calusas, who lived primarily on Florida's southwest coast, down the Keys until they ran out of land. Key West would have been their last stand. One hitch in this theory is that the Tequestas were thought to have been relatively peaceful, while the Calusas were thought to have been warlike. Also, by the time this battle was likely to have taken place, the Tequestas' numbers had dwindled considerably due to diseases brought over by Spanish explorers.

Another theory claims that the invaders were Carib Indians, who came from islands south of the Keys, perhaps present-day Cuba or Haiti and the Dominican Republic. The Caribs are known to have been cannibalistic and were even more vicious warriors than the Calusas. Were those bones on the shore of Key West not only the remains of a battle between the Caribs and the Calusas, but also the remains of the victory feast that followed?

In 1815, for reasons unspecified, the then-Spanish governor of Florida gave Cayo Hueso to Juan Pablo Salas, a Spanish military officer. Seven years later, one year after the United States acquired Florida from Spain, Salas attempted to sell the island to two different people. First, he traded it to an unnamed sailor in exchange for the sailor's sloop. Then, in a bar in Havana, he sold it to a Mobile, Alabama, businessman named John Simonton for $2,000. Simonton won the ensuing dispute over ownership. He immediately sold off three-quarters of the island, one quarter to John Fleming, a friend and business associate, and the other two quarters to John Whitehead and Pardon Greene. The four owners were Key West's first developers, opening a salt mine and importing cattle and hogs. They also recognized its importance as a port and as a strategic military location. Simonton invited the United States Navy to consider building a base here, and he ended up with more than he bargained

BRUCE HUNT

Marquesa Hotel,
Key West

for. In 1822, the Navy built a base on Key West to conquer pirates who frequented these waters. The Navy put the base under the command of Commodore David Porter. Porter promptly declared himself the virtual ruler of Key West, appropriating equipment and property without permission whenever he wished. Locals labeled him a tyrant, but by 1826, he had indeed driven the pirates out of the surrounding seas.

A century after the Spanish began calling Key West the Island of Bones, the moniker was still appropriate, considering that its biggest money crop in the early 1800s was the remains (or bones, if you will) of ships smashed on the surrounding reefs. The very dangerous and perfectly legal industry was called wrecking. Brave Key Westers made a healthy living salvaging the cargoes of wrecked ships. At first, wrecking was an every-man-for-himself endeavor, but in 1828, the United States courts stepped in to regulate it. Wreckers and their ships had to acquire a license. A maritime court, established in Key West, decided how the proceeds of salvages were disbursed. This did not, however, stifle the wrecking industry. In fact, it was the beginning of its Golden Era. Through the 1830s, Key West may have been the richest city per capita in the United States.

But the good times would not last forever. In the 1850s, the United States government began erecting lighthouses along the reefs in the Keys and the wrecking business faded. In 1921, the Wrecking License Bureau closed.

Key West has long attracted artists and writers. John Audubon lived and painted here briefly in the early 1830s. Tennessee Williams came in the 1930s and wrote, among many other classics, *Cat on a Hot Tin Roof* and *A Streetcar Named Desire*. Robert Frost, Wallace Stevens, James Herlihy, Thomas McGuane, and Winslow Homer are just a few of the other famous names found at one time or another in Key West. Without doubt, Key West's most famous resident writer was Ernest Hemingway, who lived on the island from 1928 to 1940. Between afternoon fishing expeditions and all-night bar expeditions, he produced some of his best-known works, including *A Farewell to Arms* and *To Have and Have Not*. I highly recommend a visit to the Hemingway House on Whitehead Street, where he lived from 1931 until 1940.

The Marquesa Hotel
600 Fleming Street
Key West, Florida 33040
(305) 292-1919
(800) 869-4631
(305) 292-2121 fax
 (305) 292-1244 Cafe Marquesa
www.marquesa.com

27 rooms, $155–380
two pools, gourmet restaurant, non-smoking

MOST EVERYONE IN KEY West is watching the sunset from Mallory Square, but I'm watching it from the comfort of a cozy rocking chair on our room's private second-floor balcony at the Marquesa Hotel. A biplane pulling a banner that reads "2 fly for $40, 254-TOUR" just flew across that setting sun.

Cafe Marquesa and the main building of the Marquesa Hotel, at the corner of Simonton and Fleming Streets, were originally the home of Key West butcher James Haskins. He built it in 1884 and a few years later decided to lease out the downstairs portion. It was a gentleman's clothing store initially, then in 1893, it became Dr. Burgos' pharmacy. Later, it was an office for the Key West Gas Company, and in the late 1930s and 1940s, it housed a longtime Key West landmark, Fausto's Grocery Store. The current side wing of the hotel was originally a boarding house. The last Haskin family member to own the property left it to an order of Catholic nuns.

In 1987, Erik deBoer and Richard Manley purchased the building and spent nearly $1.5 million to restore it and add another wing. In 1993, they bought the two adjacent buildings and spent an additional $2.2 million to renovate them and integrate them with the existing buildings. They've included every conceivable modern convenience without detracting from the century-old charm of the place.

Loretta and I are in room #10 in the main building at the top of the stairs. It's a corner room painted a light shade of sky blue. Afternoon light filters through the gumbo limbo tree that grows next to the side window and gives the room an outdoorslike glow. While not quite as large as some of the Marquesa's other rooms, this one has an added feature: its own twenty-one-foot-long (longer than the room) balcony, with a wicker rocker and a take-a-nap-in-it, comfy, wicker love seat with deep, overstuffed cushions. The room and the balcony overlook the neighborhood on tree-shaded Fleming Street.

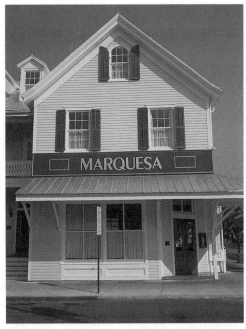

The Marquesa Hotel

The Marquesa Hotel's courtyard has two swimming pools and a waterfall surrounded by a botanical wonderland filled with exotic palms, hibiscus, ferns, and orchids. Manley and deBoer's construction contracting experience shows in this impeccable restoration.

The Marquesa is technically a hotel, not a bed & breakfast (breakfast is $7.50 extra), but it has all the warmth, appeal, and personal attention of the finest bed & breakfasts. Upon check-in, we were asked which newspapers—the local Key West paper, the *Miami Herald,* and *USA Today*—we wanted left at our door in the morning. Each afternoon, a fresh-cut orchid appeared on our nightstand.

The most difficult decision a visitor to Key West has to make is where to have dinner. Choose the Cafe Marquesa and you will never be disappointed. It is arguably the best restaurant on the island, and it is unquestionably my favorite. The menu changes daily, but to give you an idea of their fare, I started with a cup of vichyssoise with flying fish roe. My entrée was sesame-crusted yellowtail snapper in a mango sauce. It came with sautéed spinach with pineapple-chili salsa. Loretta had grilled sea scallops with citrus fruit butter, Peruvian mashed potatoes, and asparagus with tomatillo salsa. They also serve a wonderful, crisp flat bread with hummus spread made from garlic, yogurt, lime juice, and cilantro.

The Curry Mansion

511 Caroline Street
Key West, Florida 33040
(305) 294-5349
(800) 253-3466
www.currymansion.com
frontdesk@currymansion.com

28 rooms, $125–275
full breakfast, happy hour, pool

WHEN I PASS THROUGH the wrought-iron gate at the Curry Mansion, I feel like I've stepped back in time one hundred years. The Curry name is synonymous with Key West's golden era, a time when adventurers populated the island.

Wrecking, the salvaging of cargo from ships foundered on the reefs, had turned Key West into one of the richest cities per capita in the United States by the mid-1800s, and some did well in businesses that provisioned the wrecking industry. One such entrepreneur was William Curry, most certainly Key West's—and quite possibly Florida's—first millionaire.

Curry's ancestors were Scottish Loyalists forced to abandon their Carolina plantation during the Revolutionary War. Eventually, they ended up in the Bahamas. In 1837, sixteen-year-old Curry left his family's home in Green Turtle Cay for the promise of fortunes to be made in Key West. He found work as a clerk at Weever and Baldwin Mercantile for a dollar a week plus room and board. A year and a half later, he went to work for the United States Quartermaster's Office.

His work experience was his only education, but the ambitious young Curry managed to open his own business, with partner G. L. Bowne, in 1845. Bowne and Curry dealt in vessel supplies and outfitting connected with the wrecking industry. Curry's father-in-law, wrecking captain John Lowe, became the third partner when he brought his wrecking schooner, *Lavinia,* into the business. Despite an 1846 hurricane that nearly wiped them out, theirs was a successful venture that expanded to operate a fleet of wrecking schooners. By the 1850s, William Curry was the wealthiest man in the Keys and had broadened his interests to include banking, tugboats, and an icehouse. In 1861, he bought out his partners and renamed the business Curry and Sons.

Nearly all historical accounts describe William Curry as a respected community leader, a sharp businessman, and an uncanny stock market investor— despite the fact that he lived sixteen hundred miles south of New York. He is

The Curry Mansion

also described as generous, gentle, and unpretentious. His one extravagance was that, in 1880, he walked into Tiffany's in New York and ordered twenty-four complete place settings in solid 18-carat gold. When Curry died in 1896, seventy carriages accompanied his funeral procession.

Son Milton inherited the family homestead on Caroline Street, originally built in 1855. Milton's wife, Elaine, the daughter of a local banker, apparently felt that the Curry home was too modest. In 1905, she ordered it remodeled. By the time she was through with it, nothing remained of the original home except the kitchen.

Elaine Curry certainly had good taste. The mansion is a grand and ornate three-story structure that borrows its Colonial Revival style from a Newport, Rhode Island, "cottage" that Milton and Elaine saw while on their honeymoon. Other Curry Mansion architectural motifs reflect the Key West style of that era: a mixture of New England, Bahamian/Caribbean, and nautical influences. Shipbuilding carpenters constructed most of the early Key West homes, whose gingerbread trim often reflects their seafarer-style craftsmanship. It was not unusual for those craftsmen to reuse wood and other salvaged pieces (brass railings and portholes, for instance) from wrecked ships in the houses they built.

Today, the Curry Mansion is white, and its intricate exterior scrollwork is trimmed in gold. It has a pattern-stamped tin roof. Six columns flank the broad stone steps that lead from the circular brick drive onto the first-floor verandah to the double-door front entryway. The house oozes tropical grandeur. Exterior, top-hinged Bahamian shutters keep the sun out but let the breeze blow through. Many of the windows have beveled leaded glass. Wicker rockers, tables, and chairs occupy both the first- and second-floor verandahs. Rich maple paneling covers the interior walls. A rooftop cupola, or "poop deck," accessible by ladder from the third floor, offers a 360-degree view of the island and surrounding ocean. Milton probably kept watch on the family fleet from here.

Al and Edith Amsterdam, owners since 1973, operate the Curry Mansion as a bed & breakfast and also as a museum. They've furnished and decorated it with nineteenth- and early twentieth–century antiques, some acquired from around Key West, others collected from their own families. They seem to have an affinity for antique telephones and pianos. Among these is an 1853 Chickering piano once owned by author Henry James.

The original mansion has four guest rooms. There are also sixteen rooms in a 1985 addition behind the mansion and eight rooms in a house across the street that the Amsterdams restored in 1993 and opened in 1994.

Edith's poodle, Peggy, greets me from the staircase landing as I head up to room #206, the Owner's Suite. It occupies the west half of the second floor in the original mansion. Edith and Al lived in it for many years before moving across the hall. A king-size four-poster canopied bed (covered with a different handmade quilt each day) backs up to a bay window in the master bedroom. The room's antique furnishings include marble-topped bedside tables and a marble-topped dresser. Double French doors open onto the huge private verandah. There is also a sitting room and a spacious bathroom with separate shower and Jacuzzi tub.

Just outside the door is a very old George A. Prince & Company "melodeon," a small reed organ. Prince & Company manufactured melodeons from 1847 to 1866. That makes this one more than 130 years old. It's currently being restored.

Breakfast is a help-yourself affair in the courtyard and pool area between the main house and the addition. It consists of fresh-squeezed juices, cereals, bagels, Danish, croissants, and Edith's exceptional muffins and breakfast breads. My favorites are her orange and apple breads, jalapeno cornbread, and cherry muffins. The courtyard is also the gathering spot for pre-sunset happy hour, when piano player Dave plays old standards such as "As Time Goes By."

The Amsterdams accommodate nearly every whim and manage to do so without hovering over their guests. When I asked about bicycles, they had Conch Bike Express bring some to the house. A stay at Curry Mansion also includes access to guest amenities at the Casa Marina and the Pier House.

While I did not eat off of solid gold plates, it was still a luxurious treat to stay in the historic home of Key West's most prominent, turn-of-the-century family.

The Wyndham Casa Marina

1500 Reynolds Street
Key West, Florida 33040
(305) 296-3535
(305) 296-4633 fax
(800) 626-0777
(877) 999-3223
wcmbh@wyndham.com
www.wyndham.com
www.casamarinakeywest.com

239 rooms and 71 suites, $149–355
tennis courts, health club and spa, two pools, bicycles, mopeds, kayaks, handicap-accessible rooms, non-smoking rooms

THE CASA MARINA WAS to be railroad magnate Henry Flagler's last hotel, but he never got to see the groundbreaking. Construction began in 1918 and was completed in 1921, eight years after Flagler's death. (See A Tale of Two Henrys.) It is the oldest operating hotel in Key West.

Marriott purchased and thoroughly restored the three-story hotel in 1978. In 1999, the Wyndham Hotel chain bought it.

Cypress House

601 Caroline Street
Key West, Florida 33040
(305) 294-6969
(800) 525-2488
(305) 296-1174 fax
cypresskw@aol.com
www.cypresshousekw.com

16 rooms, $99–270
Continental breakfast, happy hour, pool, no children, non-smoking,
shared baths in some rooms, resident cat and dog, Sassy and Ben

THIS 1887 MANSION WAS originally the home of naturalist Richard M.
Kemp, who identified and named the Kemp sea turtle. The house is easy to
spot because its exterior has been left unpainted, as was the case with many
of the houses on Key West prior to the turn of the twentieth century.

La Mer Hotel and Dewey House

506 and 504 South Street
Key West, Florida 33040
(305) 296-6577
(800) 354-4455
lamerdewey@aol.com
www.oldtownresorts.com

11 rooms in La Mer, 8 in Dewey House, $130–315
Continental breakfast, private beach, pool, kitchenettes in some rooms

THESE TWO LUXURIOUS MANSIONS at the southern (quiet) end of
Duval Street are operated by Old Town Resorts, which also operates the South
Beach Oceanfront Motel and the Southernmost Motel. The Dewey House
was built in 1906 and was the home of philosopher and educator John Dewey.
The La Mer Hotel next door was a circa-1910 house built by architect D. B.
Walker as his home. Guests can walk out of the open and airy lobby of
either building onto their own private beach.

La Mer Hotel and Dewey House

Conch House

625 Truman Avenue
Key West, Florida 33040
(305) 293-8447
(800) 207-5806
www.conchhouse.com
conchinn@aol.com

8 rooms, $98–198
Continental breakfast

THIS TWO-STORY HOME was originally built in 1889 and restored in 1993. Carlos Recio, friend and aid to Cuban revolutionary José Marti, purchased it in 1895. Since then it has remained in successive generations of his family. Today, the Conch House is owned and operated by Recio's great-granddaughter Francine Holland and his great-great-grandson Sam Holland. There are five rooms in the main house and three more in the adjacent poolside cottage.

Red Rooster Inn

Red Rooster Inn
709 Truman Avenue
Key West, Florida 33040
(305) 296-6558
(800) 845-0825
(305) 296-4822 fax
chelseahse@aol.com
www.redroosterinn.com

13 rooms plus third-floor 3-bedroom suite, $79–189
Continental breakfast, pool, coffee/espresso bar

THIS THREE-STORY HOUSE, built in 1870, is known historically as the Peter H. Hanlon House, whose namesake purchased it in 1904 for $2,500. In the 1970s, it was a boardinghouse called the Cinderella Motel, frequented by Coast Guard and military personnel. The owners also own the Chelsea House next door.

Chelsea House

707 Truman Avenue
Key West, Florida 33040
(305) 296-2211
(800) 845-8859
(305) 296-4822 fax
chelseahse@aol.com
www.redroosterinn.com/chelsea/about.htm

20 rooms and suites, $75–260
Continental breakfast, pool, coffee/espresso bar (next door),
pets welcome

GEORGE L. LOWE, A well-respected banker whose family was in the mercantile and lumber business, built this house in 1891. The Chelsea House owners also own the Red Rooster Inn next door.

The Mermaid & The Alligator

729 Truman Avenue
Key West, Florida 33040
(305) 294-1894
(800) 773-1894
mermaid@joy.net
www.kwmermaid.com

4 rooms, $98–198
children over 16 welcome,
non-smoking

The Mermaid & the Alligator

THIS THREE-STORY 1904 Conch house, with wraparound first- and second-floor verandahs, sits in a lush, tropical garden setting. The unusual name comes from the Wilbur Thomas sculpture in the garden. The Treetop Suite, tucked beneath the roof gable on the third floor, has vaulted ceilings and a splendid view across Old Town Key West.

The Artist House

The Artist House
534 Eaton Street
Key West, Florida 33040
(305) 296-3977
(800) 582-7882
(305) 296-3210 fax
info@artisthousekeywest.com
www.artisthousekeywest.com

7 rooms and suites, 7 villas (a block away), $119–299
Continental breakfast with rooms and suites (but not with villas),
non-smoking, no children, pool

THIS IS PROBABLY THE most photographed house in Key West. It is a
beautifully restored 1890 Victorian, complete with turret, on a quiet side
street. Pharmacist Thomas Otto built it in 1898. Artist Gene Otto (hence the
name) lived here until his death in 1974.

The most popular room, the Turret Suite, is on two levels. Downstairs, it has a king-size four-poster bed. French doors open onto a private porch. A winding staircase leads up into the octagonal turret with its own antique bed.

Authors of Key West Guesthouse
725 White Street
Key West, Florida 33040
(305) 294-7381
(800) 898-6909
(305) 294-0920 fax
lionxsx@aol.com
www.authors-keywest.com

10 rooms, $99–295
full breakfast, no children

THERE IS VERY LITTLE from the outside to indicate that this is a bed & breakfast. The sign is so discreet that I almost didn't notice it. Authors is actually two circa-1910 Conch houses. It has a very private, tucked-away atmosphere. Each of the ten rooms is named for a famous writer who has resided in Key West. Owners Gary Johnson and Charles Candler are former art gallery owners.

Whispers Bed & Breakfast
409 William Street
Key West, Florida 33040
(305) 294-5969
(800) 856-7444
(305) 294-3899 fax
bbwhispers@aol.com
www.whispersbb.com

8 rooms, $80–160
full breakfast

THE REAR SECTION OF this three-story house dates to the 1840s. Gideon Lowe, son of one of Key West's earliest settlers from the Bahamas, built it. The front portion of the house was added in the 1860s.

Duval House

815 Duval Street
Key West, Florida 33040
(305) 292-1666
(800) 223-8825
(305) 292-1701 fax
duvalhs@attglobal.net
http://kwflorida.com/duvalhse.html

27 rooms and 3 suites, $90–325
Continental breakfast, pool, kitchenettes in suites

Tropical Inn

812 Duval Street
Key West, Florida 33040
(305) 294-9977
(305) 292-1656 fax
tropicalinn@aol.com
www.tropicalinn.com

7 rooms in main house, 2 suites in adjacent cottage, $109–249
Continental breakfast, non-smoking, no children

Center Court Historic Inn and Cottages

916 Center Street
Key West, Florida 33040
(305) 296-9292
(800) 797-8787
www.centercourtkw.com

6 rooms in main house plus 11 cottages, $88–358
rooms include breakfast (cottages do not), pets welcome with $10 fee,
main house built in 1880, resident Jack Russell terrier and black Lab

Paradise Inn

819 Simonton Street
Key West, Florida 33040
(305) 293-8007
(800) 888-9648
paradise@keysdigital.com
www.theparadiseinn.com

15 suites and 3 cottages, $175–350
Continental breakfast, pool, room service from Thai restaurant next
door, old Conch-style architecture but new construction (built in 1996)

Merlinn Inn
811 Simonton Street
Key West, Florida 33040
(305) 296-3336
(800) 642-4753
merlinnc@aol.com
www.merlinnkeywest.com

11 rooms, 5 suites, 4 cottages, $89–235
full breakfast, non-smoking, kitchens in four units,
resident parrots living in courtyard

Courtney's Place
720 Whitmarsh Lane
Key West, Florida 33040
(305) 294-3480
(800) 869-4639
cplacekw@keysdigital.com
www.keywest.com/courtney.html

6 rooms, 6 cottages, 2 efficiencies, $79–199
pets allowed, highest elevation in Key West
(eighteen feet above sea level), named after
Courtney Krumel, daughter of the owners

The Colony
714 Olivia Street
Key West, Florida 33040
(305) 294-6691
(305) 294-0402 fax
www.thecolonykeywest.com

individual cottages, $875–1,330 weekly
full kitchens, private decks, pool, no college spring-breakers

Blue Parrot Inn
916 Elizabeth Street
Key West, Florida 33040
(305) 296-0033
(800) 231-2473
bluparotin@aol.com
www.blueparrotinn.com

10 rooms, $79–179
full breakfast, pool, children over 16 welcome, 1884 house built by
Walter Maloney, former Key West mayor and editor of Key West
Dispatch, six resident cats

Heron House
512 Simonton Street
Key West, Florida 33040
(305) 294-9227
(888) 861-9066
heronkyw@aol.com
www.heronhouse.com

18 rooms and suites, $119–349
Continental breakfast, pool, orchid nursery, sunning decks
in three upstairs suites, original house built in 1856

Key Lime Inn
725 Truman Avenue
Key West, Florida 33040
(305) 294-5229
(305) 294-9623 fax
(800) 549-4430
www.keylimeinn.com

37 cabana rooms and cottages, $99–255
full breakfast, pool, non-smoking, opened in 1999,
original house built in 1854

Coconut Beach Resort
500 Albert Street
Key West, Florida 33040
(305) 294-0057
(800) 835-0055
(305) 294-5066 fax
www.coconutbeachresort.com

32 one- and two-bedroom suites, $160–450
pool, private beach

Island City House
411 William Street
Key West, Florida 33040
(305) 294-5702
(800) 634-8230
(305) 294-1289 fax
islcity@flakeysol.com
www.islandcityhouse.com

24 rooms and suites, $115–315
fullbreakfast, pool, bicycles, two restored and one completely
rebuilt circa-1880 houses, originally
converted to hotel in 1906

Bananas Foster Bed & Breakfast
537 Caroline Street
Key West, Florida 33040
(305) 294-9061
(800) 653-4888
(305) 292-9411 fax
bananaf@bellsouth.net
www.bananasfoster.com

6 rooms, 1 suite, $110–310
Continental breakfast, 1886 house restored in 1994
by Foster Meagher

INDEX

If you enjoyed reading this book, here are some other books from Pineapple Press on related topics. For a complete catalog, write to: Pineapple Press, P.O. Box 3899, Sarasota, FL 34230 or call 1-800-PINEAPL (746-3275). Or visit our website at www.pineapplepress.com.

Book Lover's Guide to Florida edited by Kevin M. McCarthy. Exhaustive survey of writers, books, and literary sites. A reference, guide for reading, and literary tour guide. ISBN 1-56164-012-3 9 (hb), ISBN 1-56164-021-2 (pb)

Florida Island Hopping: The West Coast by Chelle Koster Walton. The first tour guide to Florida's Gulf coast barrier islands, including a discussion of their histories, unique characters, and complete information on natural attractions, shopping, touring, and other diversions. ISBN 1-56164-081-6 (pb)

Guide to Florida Historical Walking Tours by Roberta Sandler. Put on your walking shoes and experience the heart of Florida's people, history, and architecture as you take a healthful, entertaining stroll through 32 historic neighborhoods. ISBN 1-56164-105-7 (pb)

Hemingway's Key West by Stuart McIver. A rousing, true-to-life portrait of Hemingway the man and the writer in 1930s Key West. Includes a two-hour walking tour of Ernest Hemingway's favorite haunts. SBN 1-56164-035-2 (pb)

Historic Homes of Florida by Laura Stewart and Susanne Hupp. Seventy-four notable dwellings throughout the state tell the human side of history. All are open to the public and each is illustrated by H. Patrick Reed or Nan E. Wilson. ISBN 1-56164-085-9 (pb)

Houses of Key West by Alex Caemmerer. Eyebrow houses, shotgun houses, Conch Victorians, and many more styles illustrated with lavish color photographs and complemented by anecdotes about old Key West. ISBN 1-56164-009-3 (pb)

Houses of St. Augustine by David Nolan. A history of the city told through its buildings, from the earliest coquina structures, through the Colonial and Victorian times, to the modern era. Color photographs and original watercolors. ISBN 1-56164-0697 (hb), ISBN 1-56164-075-1 (pb)

Visiting Small-Town Florida, Volumes 1 and 2, by Bruce Hunt. From Carrabelle to Bokeelia, these out-of-the-way but fascinating destinations are well worth a side trip or weekend excursion. Vol. 1: ISBN 1-56164-128-6 (pb); Vol. 2: ISBN 1-56164-180-4 (pb)